Routledge Revivals

The Record of the National Government

The introduction of the National Government in 1931 came about due to the Wall Street Crash leading to a British Government run by members of all parties, more commonly known as a coalition government today. With public opinion split on how to deal with the financial crisis, this was initially seen as a positive step by many, but for many, the national government was not the ideal solution. Ramsay Muir was one such ex-supporter and originally published in 1936, his study aims to provide a timeline of the events happening before, during and after the original national government and how this impacted on British politics. This title will be of interest to students of Politics and Political History.

The Record of the National Government

Ramsay Muir

Routledge
Taylor & Francis Group

First published in 1936
by George Allen & Unwin Ltd

This edition first published in 2016 by Routledge
2 Park Square, Milton Park, Abingdon, Oxon, OX14 4RN
and by Routledge
711 Third Avenue, New York, NY 10017

Routledge is an imprint of the Taylor & Francis Group, an informa business

© 1936 Ramsay Muir

All rights reserved. No part of this book may be reprinted or reproduced or utilised in any form or by any electronic, mechanical, or other means, now known or hereafter invented, including photocopying and recording, or in any information storage or retrieval system, without permission in writing from the publishers.

Publisher's Note
The publisher has gone to great lengths to ensure the quality of this reprint but points out that some imperfections in the original copies may be apparent.

Disclaimer
The publisher has made every effort to trace copyright holders and welcomes correspondence from those they have been unable to contact.

A Library of Congress record exists under LC control number: 37002916

ISBN 13: 978-1-138-64349-9 (hbk)
ISBN 13: 978-1-315-62935-3 (ebk)
ISBN 13: 978-1-138-64352-9 (pbk)

The
RECORD
OF THE
NATIONAL
GOVERNMENT

by

RAMSAY
MUIR

London
GEORGE ALLEN & UNWIN LTD

FIRST PUBLISHED IN 1936

All rights reserved

PRINTED IN GREAT BRITAIN BY
UNWIN BROTHERS LTD., WOKING

CONTENTS

CHAPTER		PAGE
I.	Antecedents	9
	I. The World Crisis	
	II. Blunders of British Policy	
	III. The Financial Crisis of 1931	
II.	The First National Government	27
	I. Conditions of its Formation	
	II. Its Work	
	III. Its Premature Termination	
III.	The General Election of 1931	40
	I. Character of the Election	
	II. Its Consequences	
IV.	The Second National Government	50
	I. Conversion and Protection	
	II. Trade Revival	
	III. The Economic Conference	
	IV. Restrictions of Freedom	
	V. India and Ireland	
	VI. Foreign Policy	
V.	National Finance	73
	I. The Chamberlain Budgets	
	II. Increase of Taxation	
	III. Currency Policy and Control of Capital	
VI.	Unemployment Policy	86
	I. Unemployment Relief	
	II. Provision of Work	
	III. The Special Areas	

CHAPTER		PAGE
VII.	The Effects of Protectionist Policy	98

      I. The Balance of Trade
      II. Protection and Unemployment
      III. Protection and Efficiency
      IV. Tariffs for Bargaining

VIII.	Agricultural Policy	131

IX.	The Ottawa Agreements	143

      I. Effects upon British and Imperial Trade
      II. Effects upon the World Situation

X.	Foreign Policy	161

      I. The Main International Problem
      II. The Outstanding Issues in 1931
      III. Japan and China
      IV. The Disarmament Conference
      V. Nazi Germany
      VI. The Peace Ballot
      VII. Italy and Abyssinia
      VIII. Failure of British Policy

	Index	201

PREFACE

THIS little book is an attempt to survey the work of the National Government from the point of view of one who began by supporting it, and has been driven into more and more complete opposition. Although I have tried to give it credit for whatever it has done that is good, I do not pretend to be impartial. As a student of modern history, I believe it to be the worst, the weakest, the most timorous, and the most incompetent Government that Britain has known since the days of Lord North. Honestly holding this view, I have felt myself under an obligation to express it. But I have avoided personalities and mere denunciation. I have confined myself to the analysis of facts and to the development of serious argument. The book might have been more lively if I had adopted another method. But I submit that both the facts and the arguments deserve to be seriously weighed by those who have hitherto been bemused by the name of the *National* Government. Its worst failures have indeed been due to the *Nationalism* of its policy and to its abandonment or reversal of the principles upon which the greatness of Britain was built during the nineteenth century.

RAMSAY MUIR

THE RECORD OF
THE NATIONAL GOVERNMENT

CHAPTER I

ANTECEDENTS

THE experiment of "national" or all-party government was set on foot in Britain in 1931 as a means of enabling the country to extricate herself from the financial crisis of that year, which threatened to destroy her credit and to plunge her in financial confusion. It is impossible to form a fair judgment upon the character and results of this experiment without first obtaining clear ideas about the crisis which gave it birth.

I

Although the crisis only began to mature towards the close of 1929, it had been long in preparation, and was in truth the outcome of the dislocation of world trade and finance which had resulted from the Great War. Three aspects of this dislocation deserve to be kept in mind.

In the first place, during the war the great industrial nations of Europe, which had previously supplied the greater part of the world with the manufactured goods they required, were all so engrossed in the war that they could no longer carry on their foreign trade on the old scale. The result was that the United States and Japan saw a great increase of their foreign trade, while in many countries new manufacturing industries were stimulated into existence. When the war was over, reluctant to lose their war-time advantage, these countries protected their new industries with high tariffs. And another motive reinforced this tendency. With the experience of the war before them, most countries feared to see themselves dependent upon other countries for important classes of goods, and especially for commodities needed in war. They strove after self-sufficiency. From these causes arose the plague of "economic nationalism," which has brought distress to all countries and impoverished millions of people. It did not reach its height until the crisis which began in 1929, but it was at work earlier. The channels of world-trade were being clogged; and the peoples of the earth were being impoverished, and prevented by their Governments from enjoying the abundance which the generosity of Nature and the ingenuity of man were making available for their use.

In the second place, the war had brought about a complete disorganisation of the monetary system of all the belligerent countries, and, indeed, of others also. Before the war all the great trading countries except China had put their money on the Gold Standard: that is to say, they had guaranteed that their units of money (pound, franc, dollar, mark, etc.) should always be equal in value to a fixed weight of gold; and to ensure this their banks were always ready to give gold in exchange for their notes. But in war so much money had to be issued for the payment of troops and the purchase of supplies that all the belligerent countries had to abandon the Gold Standard and issue inconvertible paper money. Some countries were more reckless than others in their use of the printing-press for the creation of money. But all had to increase vastly their supply of money, with the result that prices rose rapidly: for when money was plentiful, more of it had to be given in exchange for the same amount of goods. After the war the issue of paper money went on for the purposes of reconstruction and (in the case of Germany) under the pressure of the immense burdens imposed upon her by the victorious Allies. In some countries inflation was carried to such a point that their money became almost valueless. The result was that as the value of various countries' money changed violently from day to day, trade became almost impossible. By an immense effort this ruinous process was brought to an end in 1924 and the following years, when, in modified form, all the European countries returned to the Gold Standard. This was the chief cause of the revival of international trade which marked the years 1924-9; trade again became possible when the moneys of various countries had a fixed value in relation to one another. But vast losses had been inflicted upon certain classes of the community in the countries where this frenzied process of "inflation" had been carried furthest. All savings invested in securities with a fixed rate of interest lost value; the German (for example) who had owned £10,000 worth of national debt found that his holding was only worth a minute fraction of a penny, and in this way the German national debt was wiped out, and a large part of the German, Austrian, Polish, Hungarian, and (in a less degree) French middle classes were reduced to poverty or even destitution.

In the third place, the war left a bewildering problem of international debts. Germany owed colossal and (until 1924) undefined sums to the victorious allies (other than America) as reparations for war losses.

France, Italy, and other allied countries owed huge sums to Britain and America for supplies obtained to carry on the war; and Britain owed a vast sum to America. If these debts could all have been paid, America would have drawn gigantic sums from Europe, Britain would have had a substantial balance on the right side, and the European debtors would have been ruined. But the debts could only be paid in gold or goods. They could not be paid in gold, because there was not enough gold in the world, and the debtors did not possess it—half of it was already held by America. If the debts had been paid in goods, the world would have been swamped with goods produced by the debtor countries, for which these countries would have got no return, and the trade of the creditor countries would have been destroyed. Recognising this, Britain proposed that all these debts (except German reparations) should be cancelled, as being simply part of the creditors' contribution to the war effort. In the end this, and more than this, had to be done: German reparations were practically cancelled in 1931, and all the other debts were either cancelled or repudiated. But America, in the critical years after the war, would not agree to this proposal. Britain therefore announced that she proposed to ask her allies to pay her only such proportion of their debts as would suffice, when added to the British share of German reparations, to cover her debt to America. In 1922 the British debt to America was fixed; in 1924 the amount to be paid by Germany was fixed; and in the next year or two all the other debts were also fixed. The apparent settlement of the question of international debts helped to bring about the trade-revival of 1924–9.

But the seeming prosperity of 1924-9 was unreal. These huge transfers of wealth from one country to another, without any return, could not be carried out. They were, in fact, only carried out for a few years by virtue of huge loans from America to various European countries; not loans from the American Government to the Governments of Germany and other countries, but advances—often quite reckless— by American financiers to German and other commercial concerns; but these advances indirectly provided the means of making the agreed debt payments for a few years. America was enjoying in these years an exuberant prosperity, which she thought would never cease; the loans were made out of what seemed her superfluity; but her prosperity also was unreal, as time was to show.

Meanwhile, the attempt to pay the debts was producing an unexpected result. The chief creditors were France (owing to her giant share of German reparations), America and Britain. France and America were highly protectionist countries, which meant that they made it as difficult as possible for their debtors to pay them in goods: America, indeed, raised her tariffs to prohibitive levels for this precise purpose. Accordingly there set in a drain of gold towards America and France; and the more this went on, the more difficult it became for other countries to maintain the Gold Standard, so painfully re-established. Finally the gigantic bubble of American prosperity was pricked by the New York Stock Exchange crash of October 1929. American lending came to an end; and the financial and economic crisis began which threatened Britain with the collapse of her credit, and which led to the experiment of "National" government.

II

We shall have to return presently to the immediate antecedents of the crisis. But before we do so, it is necessary to consider certain serious blunders of policy during the years before 1929 which made it more difficult for Britain to stand the crisis when it came.

The first of these was the way in which the British debt to America was fixed. This was the work of Mr. Baldwin, then Chancellor of the Exchequer in Mr. Bonar Law's Government. He went across to America in 1922 to negotiate a settlement; but instead of trying to arrange for a general adjustment of all the debts, he made a separate agreement for Britain which was so onerous in its terms that his chief, Mr. Bonar Law, almost resigned in despair when he heard of it. Since far more favourable terms were subsequently granted by America to the other European debtors, it seems probable that a much better arrangement might have been made. Perhaps Mr. Baldwin, in his easy-going way, thought that it did not matter what obligations Britain undertook, seeing that she had already announced her intention of getting from Germany and the Allies as much as, and no more than, would suffice to meet her debt to America. But he did not reflect that he was destroying the chance of getting a general adjustment, that he was putting unnecessarily high the amount which Britain would have to exact from her debtors, and that he was thereby delaying and rendering more difficult the removal of one of the chief causes of European unsettlement. In the end, Mr. Baldwin's agreement was practically (though not formally) repudiated by the National Government of which he was a principal member. The repudiation of an acknowledged debt is not an act in which Britain can take any pride.

A still more serious blunder was the way in which, and the level at which, Britain returned to the Gold Standard in 1925. The ministers responsible for this were Mr. Baldwin, then Prime Minister, and Mr. Winston Churchill, then Chancellor of the Exchequer. It was decided, without consulting Parliament, to fix the value of the pound in gold at its pre-war level; whereas France, when she came to deal with the same problem, fixed the value of the franc in gold at only one-fifth of the pre-war level. It was held that to return to the pre-war gold value of the pound would prove the financial stability of Britain to the world, by enabling "the pound to look the dollar in the face." In the event, it had exactly the opposite effect: it was because we had returned to gold at too high a level that we were driven off it in 1931. And it had other bad effects. The value or purchasing-power of the pound having been thus increased, all creditors were enriched and all debtors were impoverished; for though the number of pounds to be paid by a debtor was not altered, the value of these pounds, and the amount of work that had to be done to earn them, was increased. The burden of the national debt, and of all debentures and fixed-interest securities, was also increased; and since there was no way of reducing wages in proportion to the increased purchasing power of the pound, manufacturers found they had to make and sell more goods to meet their wages-bill, the interest on their loans, their taxes, and their rates. This meant that they had to work at a loss, or close down (thus causing unemployment), or raise their prices. If they raised their prices, they lost sales, especially abroad. Consequently export trade was crippled, and Britain failed to get her share of the general improvement in international trade that marked the years 1924-9; the districts and the industries (such as cotton, coal, and shipping) that depended upon export trade, already hard hit by the causes we have discussed, were still more seriously hurt, and these districts began to be described as the "distressed areas." At the same time, the increase in the value of the pound made it possible to get more foreign goods for a pound, especially as the foreign producer was not forced, as his British rival was by the working of the Gold Standard, to raise his prices. Imports therefore increased out of all proportion to exports, and this continued to be the case until we were driven off the Gold Standard. Protectionists attributed this growing disproportion between imports and exports to the system of free imports that still existed in Britain. They were wrong. The disproportion was due to the excessive value which had been given to the pound, and this would have operated in precisely the same way even if Britain had been a protectionist country. This tremendous blunder, for which Mr. Baldwin and Mr. Winston Churchill were responsible, not only prevented Britain from getting her proper share in the growing trade of 1924-9; it not only fostered unemployment; it not only penalised exports and put a premium upon imports; in the end it was the main factor that made Britain unable to resist the storm when it burst upon her in 1931.

A third blunder, almost as serious in its consequences, was the way in which unemployment relief was handled.

It was only in 1921 that the Unemployment Insurance Scheme was extended to cover practically the whole range of industry. This insurance scheme could only be financially sound if the benefits which it offered had been limited to those by whom, or on whose behalf, a defined number of premiums has been paid. But in the post-war slump there were many thousands of workers who had no premiums at all to their credit. They had to be provided for; but, if the insurance scheme was not to be wrecked, special provision ought to have been made for them outside of the scheme. Instead of this, they were paid standard benefits, charged on the insurance fund, under the name of Uncovenanted or Transitional Benefit; and as the insurance fund could not possibly meet these charges, they were met by borrowing on the security of the fund. This was, of course, very unsound finance. But there was some excuse for it in the first years, when almost everybody assumed that the high level of post-war unemployment was a temporary phenomenon, which would soon disappear. By 1924, however (which is generally taken as the date of the return to normal conditions), it ought to have been clear that the trouble was not going to be evanescent. Then was the time when the problem ought to have been firmly tackled; the uninsured unemployed ought to have been separated from the insured workers, and specially provided for. Mr. Baldwin's Government came into office in 1924, and held office with a commanding majority until 1929. They had some bewildered discussions of the problem. But they did not deal with it. They went on borrowing on the security of the fund, which became more and more insolvent. When the world-crisis began in 1929, and the number of the unemployed rapidly increased, the Labour Government, then in office, continued the method of the Conservatives. They may fairly be blamed for not facing up to the problem; but it was much more difficult for them to do so than for their predecessors, who must certainly bear the heavier share of responsibility. Large-scale borrowing for the relief of unemployment was one of the main things that undermined confidence in British credit abroad. It is one of the most discreditable features of recent political controversy that the Labour Party was saddled, by their Conservative critics, with the whole responsibility for not dealing with this problem at the right time. The right time was before the crisis began; that is to say, under the Government of Mr. Baldwin.

A fourth blunder—less serious than these others, but serious enough, because it added £40,000,000 per annum to the expenditure side of the Budget, and therefore made the balancing of the Budget far more difficult—was the Derating Act of 1929, the last considerable achievement of Mr. Baldwin's ministry. A relief of the burden of rating was indeed very necessary, because it was bearing with cruel severity upon the distressed areas, in which unemployment was most prevalent; and the high rates in these areas were preventing new industries from planting themselves there, where they were most needed. Rates are levied on industrial concerns, not in proportion to the profits they earn, but roughly in proportion to the size of the buildings in which they are carried on. This basis is fair enough for some purposes—for defraying the cost of services such as policing, lighting, paving, and street-cleaning, which industry would have to meet if the community did not provide the services;

and these costs do roughly correspond to the size of the building. But the basis is quite unfair for social services such as education and poor-relief. And it was mainly the burden of poor-relief, due to unemployment, that was hampering the distressed areas. The right way to deal with this problem was to transfer to the exchequer the bulk of these social charges, without interfering with what may be called the "beneficial" rates: this would at once have placed the distressed areas, in this respect, on a level with the more fortunate areas. But Mr. Baldwin's Government did not do this. They preferred (*a*) to abolish all rates on agricultural land, (*b*) to reduce the rates on all industrial concerns by three-quarters, and (*c*) to compensate the local authorities for their losses by distributing among them, according to a complicated and ridiculous formula, the sum of £40,000,000 per annum, which became a permanent burden on the exchequer. The relief of agricultural rates was bound to enure mainly to the advantage of the landowners, whose rents were increased, whenever leases fell in, by the amount saved to the tenant in rates. The reduction of industrial rates by three-quarters did scarcely anything to improve the relative position of the distressed areas; for a manufacturer seeking a site for a new factory, and having to choose between a place where the rates had been reduced from 32s. to 8s., and a place where they had been reduced from 8s. to 2s., was still quite certain to choose the second. Moreover, in the low-rated areas, the rates on industrial concerns were reduced so much that they did not even cover the service-charges which every industrial concern ought to pay. A large part—perhaps the larger part—of the £40,000,000 was wasted on subsidies to prosperous concerns in low-rated areas that stood in no need of relief; thus the brewers, whose profits amounted to £25,000,000 in the previous year, received £400,000. This scandalously improvident finance certainly helped to unbalance the Budget when the strain of the crisis came.

There were other blunders of the pre-crisis period, less serious than these, which can only be briefly referred to. One was the Sugar Beet subsidy, also initiated by Mr. Baldwin's Government, which stimulated British farmers to compete with the tropical sun by paying for home-grown sugar a subsidy equal in amount to the total for which the whole product could be sold over the counter. This not only added a new burden to the Exchequer which helped to unbalance the Budget; it also deprived us of the export-trade that had previously paid for the imported sugar; it impoverished some of our own colonies and made them unable to buy our goods; and it deprived our ships of incoming and outgoing cargoes estimated at £300,000 a year. Such, again, was Mr. Winston Churchill's raiding of the road-fund, the health insurance fund, and other special resources, which weakened our capital position in order to make a show of prosperity budgets: the raiding of the road-fund, in particular, retarded the development of our road system at the cost of the efficiency of transport, and at the same time deprived the unemployed of work which would have reduced the burden of unemployment relief. But these are trifles, in comparison with the major blunders of these years, which gravely weakened the country's power of resistance to the crisis when it came.

III

In the autumn of 1929 the crisis began, with the Stock Exchange collapse in New York; but nobody yet foresaw what was coming. Almost at the same moment Mr. Baldwin's Government gave place to a Labour Government under Mr. MacDonald. The advent of a Labour Government caused a good deal of alarm in the City, which expected incompetent and reckless finance from the Labour Party, and perhaps confidence was undermined. Yet the financial management of the Labour Government, under the charge of Mr. Snowden, was at least as cautious and orthodox as that of Mr. Churchill. Indeed, its chief defect was that it was too timid and unadventurous. It might have foreseen and prepared for the coming crisis; but it is fair to say that nobody foresaw it, certainly not the City. The Labour Government may be blamed for not having undone Mr. Baldwin's blunder in failing to stop borrowing for unemployment relief; but it did at least attempt to reduce the burden by striking off some classes of recipients of unemployment pay, such as married women, by an Anomalies Act which it demanded some courage for a Labour Government to put forward. It may also be blamed for not undoing Mr. Baldwin's greatest blunder—the overvaluation of the pound. If the pound had been devalued in 1929 or 1930, not in a panic or under pressure, but deliberately, the situation might have been saved. But the City would have been up in arms at such a suggestion; and the Labour Government paid profound deference to the City. It might have done this and that. But if we ask ourselves whether the Conservative Government would have shown greater insight or courage had its tenure of power extended over the crisis years, it can only be said that its own record gives no justification for a favourable reply. Nobody will attribute to the Labour Government of 1929–31 great qualities of leadership or statesmanship: it was timid, wavering, and incompetent. But to charge it with responsibility for the crisis into which it was plunged, partly through the blunders of its predecessors, and to suggest (as was done for electioneering purposes) that it brought the nation to the verge of ruin, is the height of injustice.

It is unnecessary to trace in detail the exciting story of the spreading menace of financial ruin that afflicted Europe during the eighteen months following the American crash, save in so far as it is necessary for the understanding of the crisis in Britain. The course of events, however, brought out very clearly the fact of the interdependence of all countries: in the face of crisis, statesmen and financiers realised this fact, as they refused to do at other times.

The first of the greater countries to feel the effects of the cessation of American lending was Germany. During the course of 1930 she was so visibly approaching bankruptcy, and her bankruptcy would so inevitably bring, perhaps revolution, and certainly financial chaos in many other countries, that the American President was impelled in the summer of 1930 to propose a moratorium of a year, during which all international debt-payments were to be suspended. The respite was welcomed with relief by the statesmen and financiers of all countries. It gave them an interval to straighten out the financial chaos of Europe. But they made no use of it until the very last moment, when, in June 1931, gathered at Lausanne, they were forced to the conclusion that Germany must in effect be relieved from the payment of reparations. But if Germany was to make no payments to them, how were the other countries, the "victorious allies," to meet their debt-charges? They agreed among themselves that these also must go; and Britain forwent further receipts from her European debtors. But America refused to agree to this cancellation; and now the full effect of Mr. Baldwin's settlement of the American debt was revealed. Britain was left under an unconditional obligation to pay a huge annual sum to America, without any counterbalancing payments from her debtors.

Meanwhile there had been published the report of a Committee (the May Committee) which had been set up to examine the state of the national finances. It showed that, quite apart from the burden of the American debt, there was likely to be a deficit in the next British Budget of about £70,000,000, which would rise to £120,000,000 in the following year. This alarming statement reinforced the already growing belief that the credit of Britain was unsound, and that she might be the next country to be threatened with bankruptcy. Her trade seemed to be declining; the excess of her imports over her exports was growing in an alarming way; and, most sensational of all, the May report disclosed the fact that she had for years been maintaining her army of unemployed workers largely on borrowed money.

Another fact, widely known among financiers, intensified this distrust of British credit. Attracted by high rates of interest, British bankers and financiers had been lending very large amounts of capital to various German concerns, and the Bank of England itself had advanced a large sum to Austria to save her principal bank from collapse. In view of the grave situation in Germany, the creditors of that country had been compelled to accept a "standstill" agreement, whereby they undertook not to claim repayment of their advances when they were due. This meant that large amounts of British capital were locked up, and unavailable.

There were large sums of money, belonging to foreign creditors of every country in the world, on deposit in London, partly because Britain was regarded as the safest country in the world, and partly for trading purposes, Britain being the financial and trading centre of the world. The owners of these deposits began to withdraw them. They did not intend to be paid in British money, which they no longer trusted. They wanted to be paid in gold, and demanded gold from the Bank of England in exchange for their British money. Or, alternatively, they would accept French or American money, these currencies being regarded as safe because of the immense stocks of gold by which they were backed. A run on the Bank of England began. It was so fierce that the Bank had to borrow £50,000,000 from the bankers of France and America in order to meet the strain. But the panic increased in intensity. It became evident that the £50,000,000 would soon be exhausted; and the French and American bankers made it clear that they would make no further loans until they were assured that the British Budget was going to be balanced, and that, in particular, the practice of financing unemployment relief by borrowing was going to be brought to an end.

This was the situation with which the Labour Government suddenly found itself faced in August

1931. They were bewildered, unhappy, and unfamiliar with the mysteries of high finance. They might have cut the knot by deciding to abandon the Gold Standard and authorising the Bank of England to pay only in British money. But this seemed too like a sort of bankruptcy and a breach of faith with foreign depositors in Britain; though it was what their successors had to do. They discussed and agreed to various forms of drastic economy, with a view to balancing the Budget. The leaders of the other parties, Mr. Baldwin and Sir Herbert Samuel, were called into consultation, and pledged themselves to support whatever steps might be necessary. But there was one thing to which the majority of the Labour ministers would not assent. They would not reduce unemployment pay. And the foreign bankers, who held the whip hand, were believed to have insisted upon just this; as did also the leaders of the other parties and the most responsible members of the Labour Government. The Labour Government consulted with the Trade Union leaders, their masters outside Parliament, and were confirmed in their decision. In the end, they threw up the sponge and resigned; and their principal leaders, joining hands with the leaders of the other parties, formed the First National Government to save the country from what seemed like financial disaster. This was on August 24, 1931.

In reality the situation was far less serious than it was made to appear. Britain's financial position was fundamentally sound, though like other countries she had suffered from the strain of the crisis. Her Budget was not more seriously unbalanced than those of other countries, France and America included. Her available resources were enormous: the rest of the world owed her no less than £4,000,000,000. All that she needed to do was to undo the blunders for which Mr. Baldwin was even more responsible than the Labour Government: to abandon the Gold Standard, or at least to devalue the pound; to put an end to borrowing for unemployment pay; and, alongside of these measures, to take the necessary steps, however unpleasant, which would make income balance expenditure. These things were quite easily done by the new National Government—the first against their will, the second and third with the general assent of the nation.

CHAPTER II

THE FIRST NATIONAL GOVERNMENT

I

THE Government which was formed on August 24, 1931, was in two respects entitled to describe itself "as a National" Government.

In the first place, it had a definite and limited objective of the highest importance to the whole nation; the balancing of the Budget and the restoration of national credit. On this object, as on the winning of the war, there could be no difference of opinion, though there might be legitimate differences and discussions as to the best way of attaining it. It is only for a definite and limited objective of this kind that the honest co-operation of parties can be obtained, without sacrifice of their essential principles.

In the second place, so long as it was pursuing this objective, it had the support of all parties. Conservatives, Liberals, and Labourites were included in the Cabinet. It is true that the majority of the Labour Party went into opposition. But their opposition was only on detail—on the question whether unemployment pay should be reduced. On nine-tenths of the Government's proposals for balancing the Budget they were in agreement; indeed, they had themselves included most of these proposals in their own economy plans. On the main objective they were in accord with the Government.

The party leaders who combined to form this Government seemed to have realised very clearly at the outset that the "National" character of the Government could not be continued after their agreed objective had been reached, and that the name "National" could not properly be used for any Government whose policy did not carry with it the assent of all parties. It was definitely laid down that the combination was to last only until the Budget had been balanced and British credit restored; that, as soon as this was achieved, all parties should regain their freedom of action; and that the next election, whenever it came, should be fought on ordinary party lines.

This was made very clear by the leaders of the three parties: at the risk of tedium, their speeches must be quoted.

In a broadcast speech delivered on August 25th, the day after the formation of the Government, the Prime Minister, Mr. Ramsay MacDonald, spoke as follows:

One thing, and one thing only, will put British credit in a position of security, and that is a scheme consisting in economics on the one side and further revenues on the other. . . . That scheme will be produced. In order to do it, a Government has been formed. It is not a Coalition Government. I would take no part in that. It is not a Government which compels any party to it to change its principles or subordinate its distinctive individuality. I would take no part in that either. It is a Government of individuals. It has been formed to do this work. If the work takes a little time, the life of the Government will be short. When that life is finished, the work of the House of Commons and the general political situation will return to where they were last week. . . . *The election which will follow will not be fought by the Government. There will be no coupons.*

The leader of the Conservative Party, Mr. Baldwin, was even more precise in a statement which he issued on the very day on which the Government was constituted.

We Conservatives have consented for a limited period of time to enter a National Government, which is to be formed for the express purpose of carrying out such measures as are required to balance the Budget and restore confidence in our national credit; *and there is no question of any permanent coalition.* The National Government has been allotted a definite task, and on its completion it is understood that Parliament will be dissolved as soon as circumstances permit, and that each of the parties should be left free to place its policy before the electors. . . . No party will be called upon to sacrifice any of the principles in which it believes.

Still clearer was Mr. Baldwin's statement to his own party four days later

It is not a Coalition. It is a co-operation of individuals . . . for the purpose of passing legislation necessary to effect economy and to balance the Budget. . . . The Government exists for no other purpose. . . . In this matter of balancing the Budget we are all agreed. . . . After that, our agreement ends, and we part company. . . . When this Parliament dissolves, when the economics are carried and the Budget is balanced, you will then have a straight fight on tariffs.

Sir Herbert Samuel, the Liberal leader, took the same line. But he evidently expected that the work to be done would take longer than Mr. MacDonald or Mr. Baldwin seemed to anticipate. Perhaps he reflected that an emergency Budget in September would not suffice, and that the National Government ought to continue until the end of the financial year, in the following spring; perhaps he considered that a conversion of high-interest national debt, for which preparations had already been made, was part of the necessary economics. Anyway, he told his followers on August 28th that:

The Government was not intended to be a long-continuing combination, still less a permanent coalition. . . . It was a temporary combination, but in his view it could not abandon the task which it had undertaken until it had seen it well on the way to completion.

In the view of Mr. Baldwin, and apparently of Mr. MacDonald, the experiment of National or All-party Government was to have a very brief duration, after which the ordinary conditions of party warfare would be renewed. Sir Herbert Samuel seems to have thought that it would have to go on rather longer. But all were agreed that the name "National" could only be applied to a Government whose policy had practically universal support; and that the National Government ought not to appeal to the country *as* a National Government. We shall see in the sequel how these undertakings were carried out.

II

The immediate task which faced the Government was promptly and efficiently tackled. In the first place, borrowing to meet the deficiency on the Unemployment Fund had to be stopped. This involved the assumption by the Exchequer of a burden which would, of course, vary with the volume of unemployment, but which was not likely to be less than £50,000,000 per annum, and might be a great deal more. This, of course, greatly increased the difficulty of balancing the Budget. For that purpose two things were necessary: a drastic reduction of expenditure and a large increase of taxation. The first was attained by an Economy Act, which provided for reductions in the pay of all Government employees, as well as of unemployed workers. The second was attained by an emergency Budget, introduced and rapidly passed in

September, which imposed heavy new taxation, notably an additional sixpence on the income-tax.

It was the declared intention of the Government to ensure that there should be "equality of sacrifice" by all classes. This ideal was not, and perhaps could not be, attained. In the first place, only those who drew their pay from Government or from public authorities had their pay reduced; this was perhaps inevitable, but it was not equality of sacrifice. In the second place, a reduction of 10 per cent in the pittance of an unemployed man or in the pay of a private soldier represented a much heavier sacrifice than a reduction of 10 per cent in the salary of a judge or a cabinet minister. In the third place, an increase of 6d. in the £ on the income-tax was a smaller burden than the 10 per cent reductions which Government employees had to endure—especially as the better-paid of these officers had to pay the extra income-tax besides suffering a reduction of their salaries. The income-tax payers were the only section of the general public called upon to contribute directly; though indirect taxation, especially on beer, fell upon other sections of the community with the inequality which indirect taxation always involves. In the fourth place, the holders of national debt, who had profited very greatly by the increased value of the £ due to the return to the Gold Standard in 1925, were not as yet called upon to make any contribution, except through the income-tax. In short, the ideal of "equality of sacrifice" so loudly proclaimed was perhaps unattainable, and was certainly not attained.

On the whole, the people accepted the sacrifice imposed upon them with exemplary fortitude. The teachers, it is true, protested against the reduction of their salaries; and there was discontent among the sailors in the navy, which led to a threat of mutiny in the fleet at Invergordon that died out when explanations were given. Exaggerated accounts of this short-lived disturbance were widely published in the foreign Press; for this, among other reasons, foreigners were slow to believe that Britain had effectually grappled with her difficulties, and the financial drain continued. Moreover, the National Government had no sooner been established than there began a vigorous agitation for an immediate General Election, fomented especially by the Conservatives, who saw, in the discredit of the Labour Party, a wonderful opportunity for securing a great advantage for their own party. There were many, both at home and abroad, who thought that an election at this moment, when the dissatisfaction with cuts and economies was at its height, might have unpredictable results, and might in particular involve the break-up of national unity. These uncertainties contributed to make foreigners sceptical for a time about the solidity of the Government's achievement, and helped to prevent a cessation of the financial drain on London.

The consequence was that, within a month of the accession of the National Government to power, the £80,000,000 which had been borrowed from France and America, immediately after the Government was formed, was exhausted; and the Bank of England had to appeal to the Government to be exempted from the obligation of redeeming its notes in gold or its equivalent. An Act in this sense was hurriedly passed; and on September 21st, exactly four weeks after the formation of the Government, Britain abandoned the Gold Standard.

In a sense this was a severe defeat; and many thought that it would be a disaster. For the necessity of maintaining the Gold Standard had been one of the principal reasons for forming a National Government, one of the principal grounds for cutting down expenses, and balancing the Budget. The most gloomy prophecies had been made as to the inevitable results of being forced off the Gold Standard: the value of British money was to decline as terribly as the value of the German mark had earlier declined; all property was to lose its value, and everybody was to be ruined. No doubt those who had made these terrifying predictions believed what they said. But they were wildly wrong: they merely displayed their inability to understand the monetary problem. There was really no comparison between the position of Germany in 1923 and the position of Britain in 1931. Germany in 1923, loaded with reparations and unable to sell her products, was insolvent. Britain in 1931 was perfectly solvent; her realisable assets were far in excess of her liabilities. What was wrong was that the real value of the pound had been greatly exaggerated when it was fixed to gold at the pre-war level by Mr. Baldwin and Mr. Winston Churchill. Unfixed from gold, it rapidly assumed its real value. Its value or purchasing power at home remained almost unchanged. But its value abroad was henceforth determined by the demand for British money in other countries for the purpose either of buying British goods or of paying debts due to British subjects.

Promptly the value of the pound in foreign countries fell to the equivalent of 16s., and later to 14s., or even 13s. What this meant was that the Englishman had to pay £1 for 16s. or 14s. worth of foreign goods, while the foreigner could buy £1 worth of British goods for the equivalent of 16s. or 14s. in his own money. The result was that British people bought fewer foreign goods, and foreign people bought more British goods: in other words, imports tended to go down, and exports to go up. The growing disproportion between imports and exports, which had been regarded as a proof of the decline of British trade, and which Protectionists had attributed to the system of free imports, was checked, and was seen to be due to the excessive value put upon the pound when it was fixed to gold, and not at all to fiscal policy. There was a rapid improvement in export trade and a decrease in unemployment, most marked in the textile trades, which especially depended upon exports. There were 100,000 fewer unemployed workers in December 1931 than there had been in December 1930. And this improvement continued until March 1932.

III

The National Government had thus, in a few weeks, done three vitally important things—two of them deliberately, the third (and the most important) very much against its will. It had stopped borrowing for current expenditure; it had balanced the Budget; and it had abandoned the Gold Standard, thus giving a fair chance to British trade, so far as a mad world would permit; and at the same time ensuring that the balance of payments between Britain and other countries would be automatically rectified by the natural fluctuations in the exchange value of the pound. It might be argued that the National Government had done its work, and that, in accordance with

THE FIRST NATIONAL GOVERNMENT

the pledges given by its leaders, the normal conflict of parties should be resumed.

But the work was not yet completed. The Budget was only balanced on paper; not until the normal Budget time came, after the close of the financial year on March 31st, could it be told whether the steps which had been taken were adequate. On that ground, it could be argued that the National Government ought to remain in office until a normal Budget had been carried.

Again, an essential element in the reorganisation of national finance had still to be carried through. The burden of the National Debt had to be tackled. Already plans were ready for the conversion of a great mass of War Loan, to the value of £2,000,000,000, from a 5 per cent to a $3\frac{1}{2}$ per cent basis. The moment was very favourable for carrying this out; for, as trade was in a bad way, holders of national debt would have difficulty in finding alternative investments, and would therefore be ready to accept a lower rate of interest rather than be paid off. The successful accomplishment of this plan, already prepared, would not only reduce very greatly the burden on the exchequer, it would also tend to reduce the general rate of interest, and thus help in the recovery of trade. It would have been a very proper thing that this conversion scheme should be carried out before the National Government wound up its work.

Finally, it was not enough that the Exchequer should assume responsibility for the annual deficit on the Unemployment Insurance Fund. The whole financial organisation of Unemployment relief had to be put upon a sound basis: the insured unemployed had to be separated from the uninsured unemployed, for whom special provision would have to be made. The neglect of previous Governments, both Conservative and Labour, to deal with this problem had in a large degree been the cause of Britain's inability to face the crisis; and it would have been right that the National Government should deal with it.

For all these reasons it seemed obvious to most people that the National Government ought to continue and complete its work, remaining in office until at least the end of the financial year, and until the unreasoning panic that had been created had time to die down.

But this was not permitted, because the Conservatives were determined to have an immediate General Election. It was contended that the country ought to be given an opportunity of expressing its judgment on the National Government. But this was not the real reason. The Conservatives had convinced themselves that the position could only be redeemed by the imposition of tariffs; they saw before them an admirable opportunity of carrying into effect a policy which they had long advocated, but which the electors had always rejected. They were alarmed by the "adverse balance of trade"—the disproportion between imports and exports—and they insisted that the restriction of imports by tariffs could alone "rectify the balance."

They could not or would not see that the disproportion between imports and exports was already being rectified by the departure from the Gold Standard: if the election had been delayed for six months this would have been obvious. They could not, or would not, see that while tariffs might reduce imports, they were bound also to reduce the exports which go to pay for them, and thus hit very hard the already hard-hit export trades; and that they were bound even more to reduce British earnings from shipping, insurance, etc., which depend upon the volume of import and export trade. In these ideas the Conservatives were strengthened by the adhesion of a certain number of Liberals hitherto convinced Free Traders—notably Sir John Simon, who made solemn speeches about the balance of trade, reviving ancient theories that had been regarded as obsolete fallacies ever since they were demolished in the eighteenth century by David Hume and Adam Smith. The Conservatives and their allies also saw that the Labour Party, their principal rivals, had lost their best-known leaders, were deeply discredited by their failure to face up to the crisis, and might be plausibly represented as responsible for its having come about. They saw that the Liberals were deeply divided by the secession of Sir John Simon and his friends, while their great popular orator, Mr. Lloyd George, was disabled by illness, and the Liberal Party exchequer was known to be empty. If they could go to the country while the panic about the crisis still survived, and if they could use the immense asset of the name of the *National* Government they could anticipate a sweeping victory. They would have been more upright than politicians often are if they had resisted these temptations.

But how were these projects to be reconciled with the Prime Minister's pledge that the National Government would not go to the country *as* a National Government, or with Mr. Baldwin's undertaking that, when the time for an election came, "each of the parties should be free to place its policy before the electors," and that there would be a straight fight on tariffs? If the Conservative plan was to be carried out these undertakings would have to be forgotten. It is fair to say that the Prime Minister seems to have had misgivings, and to have given way very reluctantly to the demand for an immediate election. Mr. Baldwin—the most astute electioneer of our time—seems to have had none.

The Cabinet, which had been limited to ten members, included four Labour, four Conservative, and two Liberal ministers: thus, as was proper in a "National" Government, no party had a majority or could impose its own will. But at least two of the Labour ministers were so full of malice against their former colleagues that they were eager to precipitate an election as a means of bringing about their downfall; and one of the two Liberal members was favourable to the idea of an early election. Despite the pledges which had been given when the National Government was formed, it was therefore decided that there should be an early election, and that it should be fought by the National Government as such.

But on what issue was the election to be fought? The Conservatives would have liked to fight it on the tariff issue; and Mr. Baldwin had promised "a straight fight on tariffs." But on this issue the National Government could not go to the country as a united body. There were long discussions in the attempt to find a formula which all could accept. At length it was decided to ask the electors for "a doctor's mandate" to do whatever might seem necessary for the restoration of the country's financial stability, without specifying any definite policy. It was agreed that the introduction of tariffs would be covered by the "doctor's mandate," if they were found to be necessary to meet an emergency; but the Liberals were given to understand that no permanent change would be made in the country's fiscal system until a "scientific and impartial inquiry" had been held.

On this basis a general election was precipitated less than two months after the formation of the Government, and before its work was completed. The component elements in the Government issued separate election addresses, the Liberals alone including in their address an assertion that, whatever measures might be necessary in an emergency, free trade was the only sound fiscal policy for the country. The election took place in October, before the panic of the previous two months had had time to subside.

CHAPTER III

THE GENERAL ELECTION OF 1931

THE election which was precipitated in October 1931 was held before the panic that had been created by the events of August and September had had time to subside, and when the electors were still bewildered by the sudden menace of financial collapse, which they did not understand. If it had been delayed until the end of the financial year, in April or May of 1932, it would have been clear that the measures already taken by the first National Government, and the further measures it would have taken between October and March, had removed all serious danger. It would also have been apparent whether or no departure from the Gold Standard had been sufficient to reduce the excess of imports. Unfortunately, as soon as the election was declared, imports began to rise again. The reason for this was that it was generally anticipated that the Conservatives would score a victory, and would then impose tariffs; and importers hastened to bring in large stocks in anticipation of the expected duties.

It should have been the duty of statesmanship to allay the public panic, and to lay before the electors a sober and reasonable view of what had happened. But panic was an electioneering asset; it was therefore fomented—an easy task, because very few really understood the mystery of money. The Prime Minister, for example, waved before his audiences specimens of German notes issued at the height of the inflation, when a 1,000,000-mark note was worth less than a penny; and suggested that, unless the National Government was returned to power, the value of British money would decline in the same way and everybody would be ruined. It is hard to believe that Mr. MacDonald can really have thought that this was true, especially after he had had a month's experience of the results of departure from the Gold Standard: if he did think so, he was manifestly incompetent to guide the country through a financial crisis. But perhaps he, like his audiences (but with far less excuse), was still under the influence of panic. If so, the criminal unwisdom of precipitating an election at this moment was once more demonstrated. From every Conservative platform this sort of argument was repeated.

In the atmosphere thus created, the appeal to vote "National," to be "patriotic," and to support the combination of parties that had united to save the country in its time of peril, was all but irresistible. An appeal of this sort is more effective if a definite "public enemy" can be indicated; and this role was assigned to the Labour Party, which had held office during the two years preceding the crisis. The fact that the Prime Minister and the Chancellor of the Exchequer in the Labour Government were also the Prime Minister and the Chancellor of the Exchequer in the National Government did not avail to qualify this attack. The charges against the Labour Party were not merely that it had been muddleheaded, incompetent, and lacking in foresight, or that it had failed to foresee and prepare for the crisis, or that it had run away from it when it came: these would have been reasonable grounds of criticism. But it was alleged that the Labour Government had actually *caused* the crisis, and had led the country (after two years of financial maladministration for which the Prime Minister and the Chancellor of the Exchequer were primarily responsible) to the very verge of ruin. This was, as we have seen, a monstrous and palpable absurdity. The crisis was in the main due to international movements which no British Government could have prevented; and Britain's inability to stand the strain when it came was in the main due to the blunders committed by previous Conservative Governments, which were analysed in an earlier chapter of this book. But in the atmosphere of panic, these assertions were readily accepted. In any other circumstances the electors would have turned to derision the preposterous contradictions that were put before them in a thousand speeches; first, that the country had been brought to the brink of disaster by two years of government under Mr. Ramsay MacDonald; and, secondly, that the only remedy for this state of things was to put blind confidence in Mr. Ramsay MacDonald and give him a blank cheque. Has there ever been another election in which such fantastic contradictions would have passed muster? They would not have been tolerated if the election had been postponed for six months.

The most remarkable argument in the campaign against the Labour Party was the assertion that they had been using the deposits in the savings bank for current expenses; it was suggested that the people's savings were not safe in the hands of a Labour Government. This assertion was first promulgated by Mr. Walter Runciman, and later adopted by Mr. Philip Snowden. Endorsed by these high authorities, it had the most profound effect: nothing did more harm to Labour candidates. Yet Mr. Runciman and Mr. Snowden must have been perfectly aware that all

Governments had always used these floating balances to diminish the amount of their borrowing before the taxes came in; that they had always paid interest on them; and that savings-bank deposits, being backed by all the credit of the State, were as safe as, or safer than, the Bank of England. That public men of standing should have used such an argument, and "got away with it," showed how truth and reason can be distorted in the heat of an election fight.

The real issues of the election were never put before the electors. What were they? Not the necessity of stopping borrowing for current expenditure or of balancing the Budget, nor the desirability or otherwise of abandoning the Gold Standard: all these questions had already been decided. Nor did anybody dream of submitting to the electors the desirability of carrying out a great conversion of War Loan: this had already been decided upon, and all preparations for it had been made; but they could not be publicly discussed. Nor was the opinion of the electors asked upon foreign policy, though the action of Japan in Manchuria was already very threatening. There was only one major question affecting the economic fortunes of the country which remained undecided—the question whether a change of fiscal policy was necessary as a means of restoring prosperity. On this question it might have been expected that the electors would be asked to give a clear verdict, especially as Mr. Baldwin had promised, when the first National Government was formed, that at the next election there should be "a straight fight on tariffs." But the issue was blurred, and there was no "straight fight."

If the election had been delayed until April or May of 1932, and this question had then been squarely put to the electors, there might have been some doubt as to their verdict. For by that time the effects of departure from the Gold Standard would have been revealed, and the disproportion between imports and exports would probably have been remedied without any resort to tariffs: by that time, also, the conversion of War Loan might have been effected, with the consequence of a lowering of the general rate of interest; and the combined effect of cheap money and the abandonment of the Gold Standard would probably have been a substantial revival of trade. In these circumstances the result of a "straight fight" on tariffs would have been by no means certain.

But in the general panic that still continued in October 1931, the result even of a "straight fight" was almost a foregone conclusion. The disproportion between imports and exports was almost universally attributed, not to its true cause, the working of the Gold Standard (which very few understood), but to the system of free imports; and it seemed plausible to contend that an excess of imports could best be checked by duties on imports. And the fact that the volume of international trade had been greatly reduced by tariffs throughout the world was widely regarded, not as a proof that tariffs had mischievous results, but as a reason why Britain should arm herself with tariffs against the tariffs of other countries. Even in a "straight fight," therefore, a protectionist victory was assured in the panic conditions of October.

There was, however, no "straight fight" on this question. Mr. Baldwin insisted that tariffs were not an issue in this election. Mr. Snowden, an unbending Free Trader, assured hesitating voters over the wireless that if the Conservatives should win a majority, they were too honourable to use it for the purpose of imposing a protectionist system on the country, and *no Conservative leader repudiated this statement*. The purpose of these pronouncements was to persuade believers in Free Trade to vote for protectionist candidates. They were highly successful. On the strength of them, millions of Liberals and Free Traders gave their votes to Conservatives and Protectionists—only to be told, later, that they had given a mandate for the introduction of a protectionist system. For every Conservative condidate, including Mr. Baldwin himself, put tariffs in the forefront of his policy.

Like Mr. Baldwin's promise that there should be a "straight fight" on tariffs, Mr. Ramsay MacDonald's promise that there should be "no *coupons*," or official recommendations of particular candidates by the Government, was forgotten in the heat of the election fight. The first letter of recommendation of this sort was issued in a case where a Liberal candidate was standing in a traditional Liberal seat against a sitting Conservative member who had won the seat on a minority vote. The Liberal candidate stood as a supporter of the National Government, but also as a Free Trader; his position was that since the National Government was not committed to a tariff policy, and since this question was bound to come up for discussion in Parliament, it was important, if the national character of the Government was to be preserved, that both sides of the argument should be effectively represented. Since there was no Labour candidate, the electors, in choosing between two supporters of the Government, ought to be free to say which side of the tariff controversy they took. Thereupon Mr. Ramsay MacDonald, as Prime Minister, sent a letter to the electors, instructing them that the Conservative sitting member must be regarded as the only legitimate "national" candidate. This letter was used in several cases of the same kind. No such official recommendation was given in cases where the sitting members were Liberals, unless (like the followers of Sir John Simon) they had beforehand given satisfactory pledges to the Conservatives. Most of the Liberal members, though supporters of the Government, were opposed by Conservatives: three minor ministers were in this way defeated. If the letters used for this purpose were not *coupons*, it is not easy to imagine what meaning is to be attached to that word.

The Conservatives entered this election, not unnaturally, full of confidence: they had a brimming exchequer, and 517 candidates in the 615 constituencies. With them were closely linked 40 Simonite candidates and 21 National Labour candidates, who had given satisfactory pledges, and who received full Conservative support.

The Labour Party, with a great effort, succeeded in putting up 513 candidates. But they were disheartened by the loss of their principal leaders, and bewildered by the vehemence of the attack directed against them. To defend themselves against the unjust charge that they had caused the crisis, they very foolishly attempted to lay the blame upon the bankers, describing the crisis as a "bankers' ramp," and urging that the State should take control of the banks. This only intensified the alarm already raised by the assertion that they had been making use of the savings bank deposits, and contributed to their undoing.

The Liberals, now the only party that adhered to Free Trade (for the Labour Party spoke on this subject with a very uncertain voice), were in an extremely weak position. One section of their party in Parliament, following Sir John Simon, had thrown in their lot with the Conservatives. Another, led by Mr. Lloyd George, declared that the election was a wicked device to destroy Free Trade by a flank attack, and went into open opposition to the Government. The main body, led by Sir Herbert Samuel, and supported by all the representative bodies of the party, strongly condemned the precipitation of the election, but still supported the National Government, while adhering to Free Trade. But their exchequer was empty; they were only able to put up candidates in one-fifth of the constituencies; and, wherever they tried to wrest seats from Conservatives, they were hamstrung by the MacDonald coupon.

II

The result of an election conducted in these conditions and by these methods was inevitable. The Conservatives swept the country, more completely than they can ever have expected. When the results were declared, it appeared that the new House of Commons included 471 Conservatives, 35 Simonites, 13 National Labourites, and 2 who called themselves simply "National." All these were pledged to a protectionist policy—a total of 521 out of 615. There were also 33 Liberals, who, while supporting the Government, adhered to Free Trade: the Government thus commanded 554 votes out of 615. On the other side were 4 Independent Liberals, led by Mr. Lloyd George, and 52 members of the Labour Party. The Labour Party was almost wiped out: with two exceptions, every Labour ex-minister was defeated, and an almost leaderless handful of inexperienced men was left to make face against the gigantic Government majority.

These astonishing figures made it appear that the whole country was united in supporting the National Government; and this no doubt produced a useful and steadying effect abroad. Making every allowance for the panic under whose influence the election was fought, it was indeed a tribute to the patriotic sentiment of the British people that they should have upheld by such overwhelming majorities a Government which had imposed upon nearly all of them such severe sacrifices. But (as always in British elections) the composition of the new House of Commons did not reflect the real balance of opinion in the country. Nearly one-third of the total votes cast had been given to the Labour Party, and if their representation had been in proportion to their electoral strength, they would have had, not 52, but 200 members. Such was the result of a ridiculous electoral system. As for the Free-Trade Liberals, there were no means of determining their electoral strength; but it was certainly far greater than the figures showed. The great majority of Liberals had no opportunity of voting for a candidate who represented their views; millions of them had voted for protectionist candidates, on the representations of Mr. Baldwin and Mr. Snowden; and they had been further handicapped by the MacDonald coupon.

The overwhelming majority thus obtained by the Government—a majority of nearly ten to one in the House of Commons—might seem to demonstrate the truly "national" character of the Government. In reality it had the opposite effect. The essence of a National Government is that it should be a combination of all parties for a specific end, without any sacrifice of the principles of any party. The only specific end upon which all parties were agreed was the balancing of the Budget, which had already been achieved before the election took place. On the strength of this achievement, the Government had obtained an overwhelming majority; but it was a majority which was entirely dominated by a single party. Before the election, the Cabinet had been so constituted that no party had a majority. After the election it was reconstituted. It now consisted of 11 Conservatives, 4 Simonites, 2 National Labourites, and 3 Liberals. The Conservatives thus had a majority of two; but since the election, and the pledges they had then given, the Simonites and the National Labourites were in effect dependent upon the Conservatives.

What is more important, the character and policy of any Government are necessarily determined by the nature of the majority which supports it in Parliament. And in Parliament there were 471 Conservatives out of 615 members. If all the Liberals, all the Simonites, and all the National Labourites had gone into opposition, and had there been joined by the handful of independents as well as by the Labour Party and the followers of Mr. Lloyd George, the Conservatives would still have had a majority of 327: they outnumbered all other sections of the House, put together, by three to one. A Government controlled by so overwhelming a majority of a single party could not be anything but a party Government; it could not, in any rational sense of the word, be a "National" Government.

In short, the election of October 1931 turned what had been a National Government into a Conservative Dictatorship.

CHAPTER IV

THE SECOND NATIONAL GOVERNMENT

The life of the second National Government extended over four years, from the General Election of 1931 to that of 1935. In succeeding chapters we shall survey its work in various spheres. In this chapter it will be convenient to consider in general terms the work of the Government as a whole. One feature of its history was the steady diminution of its "national" character and the growing preponderance of the Conservatives. At the end of the first year of its existence, its national character was impaired by the withdrawal of the small group of Liberals (the only independent group in the Government), who found it more and more difficult to submit to the complete ascendancy of the Conservatives. In the summer of 1935 Mr. Ramsay MacDonald was replaced as Prime Minister by Mr. Baldwin, and the essentially Conservative character of the ministry was still more clearly displayed. At the beginning of the period the Cabinet contained 11 Conservatives and 9 others; at the end it contained 15 Conservatives and 7 others.

I

The outstanding achievements of the first year were (1) the completion of the scheme of financial re-organisation by the successful conversion of £2,000,000,000 of public debt from a 5 per cent to a $3\frac{1}{2}$ per cent basis; and (2) the destruction of Free Trade, and the establishment in its place of a complete protectionist system, bringing Britain into line with the economic nationalism of the rest of the world.

The conversion of War Loan, which was effected in the summer of 1932, had long been prepared, and would have been carried out by the First National Government if its existence had not been cut short. It was a very remarkable achievement, which won the admiration of the world. Not only did it bring a large saving in interest to the Exchequer, of some £30,000,000 a year, but it led to a general lowering of interest charges, and inaugurated a period of "cheap money" which could not but be advantageous to industry. What made it possible, of course, was the terribly depressed condition of trade: holders of debt who were offered the alternative of accepting a reduced rate of interest or being paid off, nearly all chose the first alternative, because if their money had been refunded to them they could not have found any profitable investment for it.

The overthrow of Free Trade and the establishment of Protection had been inevitable since the General Election, in spite of the disingenuous assurance of Mr. Baldwin that this was not an issue in the election. For the whole Conservative Party had convinced itself that a tariff system would bring trade recovery, and diminish, or even put an end to, unemployment: "tariff reform," they had promised, "means work for all." The Simonites and the National Labour group had committed themselves to the same view, and had given satisfactory pledges before they secured Conservative support in the election. Only the small Liberal group remained loyal to Free Trade. It was inevitable that their resistance should be swept aside by the gigantic Conservative majority. Mr. Baldwin's pledge that "no party joining in the National Government will be called upon to sacrifice the principles in which it believes" simply could not be observed in the new conditions. The Liberals had been given to understand that, whatever emergency measures might be necessary, no permanent change in the country's fiscal system would be proposed until an "impartial and scientific inquiry" had been held; and, knowing the weakness of their position, the Liberal leaders had promised to accept emergency measures proved to be necessary, and to abide by the results of an "impartial and scientific inquiry." But no inquiry of this sort was ever set on foot.

The little group of Liberals were, in truth, in an extremely difficult position. They held it to be their duty to maintain the co-operation of parties until the purpose for which it was established had been fulfilled —until a normal Budget had shown a true balance of income and expenditure, and until the conversion of War Loan had been carried out. But if they abandoned their principles in order to maintain the façade of National Government, they would lower the standard of public life and exhaust the patience of their followers in the country. Not without misgivings, they assented to certain special and temporary duties which were imposed immediately after the election, on the ground that these were emergency measures. With still deeper misgivings, and in face of many protests from their followers, they assented to a proposal to establish a "wheat quota" for a period of three years, during which a reorganisation of agriculture was to be carried out. But when, at the beginning of 1932, without any preliminary inquiry, the Chancellor of the Exchequer introduced a general tariff of 10 per cent on almost the whole range of imports, and proposed the establishment of a Tariff Commission of three members with power to levy higher duties on any class of goods, subject only to the most formal approval by Parliament—and, still more, when this revolutionary measure was recommended not in any sense as an emergency measure, but as the fulfilment of a policy which the Conservative Party had been advocating for thirty years—the patience of the Liberals was exhausted, and, in association with Lord Snowden, they proffered their resignation.

The strongest pressure was brought to bear upon them to preserve the semblance of national unity. It was even proposed that, in contravention of all constitutional usage, they should be permitted, while remaining members of the Government, to speak and vote against the Government's principal proposals. They accepted this extraordinary arrangement, and under its terms some cogent and closely reasoned speeches were made against the new system. But it was not possible—it would not have been thought to be decent —for the Free Trade Liberals to take advantage of this indulgence so far as to fight every clause and every line of the proposals, as they would otherwise naturally have done. After having lasted during the ninety most prosperous years of British history, the system of Free Trade was destroyed without any persistent defence. Some have felt that the Liberals over-valued the importance of the contribution they could now make to the restoration of financial stability, and that they under-valued the importance of steadfast adherence to principle.

Finally, in the summer of 1932, the new protectionist system was completed by the conclusion of the Ottawa

Agreements, which we shall discuss fully in a later chapter. Even the members of the Government found it difficult to stomach these agreements; they almost returned home without signing them. This was the last turn of the screw for the Liberals, who (with Lord Snowden) resigned from the Government in October 1932, and a few months later "crossed the floor" and went into open opposition.

It might have been supposed that this would have put an end to the claim that the Government was a self-respecting combination of independent parties to pursue an agreed policy; for the Conservative Party was now the only organised party in the country which supported the Government, and it obviously controlled the situation. But the pretence was still maintained, for the name "National," however incorrectly used, was a valuable electoral asset. The Simonite Liberals had no support in the country, except in constituencies in which Simonite members had a personal hold; they were repudiated by every representative organisation of the Liberal Party, and found it impossible, until 1936, to set up any organisation of their own. The National Labour group were even more completely out of touch with the Labour Party. No member of either group could have secured election anywhere without Conservative support. They were, in fact, pensioners of the Conservative Party; and, as Mr. Baldwin very frankly said, their manifest destiny was to be absorbed in that party, as the Liberal Unionists had been, forty years earlier. There could be, and there was, no pretence that the Government was pursuing anything but a Conservative policy. But the name "National" was still preserved. It was the latest *alias* of the Conservative Party; and since unthinking people are easily influenced by names, it was an exceedingly useful *alias*.

II

The trade figures for the first fifteen months of the Government's existence showed that, instead of improving, trade was becoming rapidly worse. The improvement that had followed the departure from the Gold Standard soon slowed down, and from March 1932, when the new protectionist system came into operation, there was a rapid decline. For the whole year 1932, the total figures for British exports sank to the low level of £365 millions, as compared with £390 millions in the crisis year 1931. Unemployment increased month by month during 1932, until it reached the peak figure of 2,900,000 in January 1933 —the highest total since records began to be kept: the highest total, indeed, in British history.

Early in 1933, however, an improvement began, which went on during the remainder of the Government's term of office. The best measure of this improvement is to be found in the unemployment figures, which fell steadily until, on the eve of the General Election of 1935, they were 1,837,000. But this improvement in the figures was partly due to more severe conditions of unemployment relief which were introduced by the Government. To get a true view of the facts, we must also take into account the number of persons in receipt of out-door poor relief. This figure showed a large increase in each of the years 1933, 1934, and 1935—the years of improving trade; and by September 1935 the number had increased by over 450,000 as compared with the same month in 1931.

This increase was of course due to the fact that workers denied unemployment pay were perforce thrown back upon poor relief. Moreover, allowance must be made for what is called "black-coated" unemployment, for which no figures are available, because the "black-coated" do not receive unemployment relief. There is no doubt that a very large number of clerks and others engaged in import and export business and in shipping were thrown out of work by the restrictions upon these classes of business that were directly due to the tariff system. In short, the real improvement in unemployment was very much less than was indicated by the numbers in receipt of unemployment pay.

Such trade revival as there was during these years was almost wholly in the home trades. The export trades made very little advance. By the end of 1934, after nearly three years of the new policy, our total exports (including re-exports) were still £7 millions behind what they had been in the crisis year, 1931, £200 millions behind what they had been in 1930, and nearly £400 millions behind what they had been in 1929. And this in spite of all the advantages that were supposed to have been derived from the Ottawa Agreements. There was a substantial advance in 1935; but even then, the total was not much better than that of 1931, and £350 millions behind 1929. Whether we measure by unemployment figures or by the figures of export trade, it cannot be said that the Government had brought about any substantial improvement during its four years of office.

Such as it was, can the trade revival of these years be attributed to the policy pursued by the National Government? It probably would not have taken place but for the restoration of British credit after the shock

THE SECOND NATIONAL GOVERNMENT 57

of 1931. But that was the work of the *First* National Government. The question we have to consider is whether the modest revival of 1933–5 was due to the distinctive and Conservative policy of the *Second* National Government? An affirmative answer seems scarcely possible when we realise that during these years there was a general revival of world-trade, which was shared in by practically all countries except those that still clung to the Gold Standard; and that, according to the statisticians of the League of Nations, seven nations enjoyed a greater relative improvement than Britain. In other words, Britain was carried on the tide of a general (if slight) world-movement, and did not profit from it as much as some other countries.

Yet she ought to have done so. She had escaped from the crippling handicap of an over-valuation of her money, though other countries shared in that. But she also had the very great advantage of cheap money. If British men of business (especially those engaged in the export trades) had been told in 1930 or 1931 that the Gold Standard was going to be abandoned, and that they were going to be able to borrow all the money they required at a very low rate of interest, they would certainly have anticipated a great revival of export trade. They got these boons, and in addition they had the further advantage of a general revival of world-trade. The real question which we ought to ask ourselves is why the improvement in export trade was so pitifully small? The question seems to be, not whether the Government deserved the credit of such revival as there was, but whether it deserved the *dis*credit of this revival's smallness when circumstances were very favourable.

The chief cause of the revival of home-trade was a

remarkable activity in house-building which distinguished these years, and which, besides giving a great deal of employment in the building and furnishing trades, and in the trades that supplied them with materials, also sent a stream of money over the counters into all the trades that supplied consumable goods. This activity was only in a minor degree due to Government action: there was no large public building campaign, except for the demolition and replacement of slums at the end of the period. It was due mainly to cheap money and the falling prices of building materials, which made house-construction a profitable undertaking for private enterprise; and partly to the fact that saving, especially in the lower middle classes, was taking the form of house-purchase by instalment. Since we have never imported houses from abroad, it cannot be pretended that the building boom was due to the protectionist policy of the Government.

It is certain, however, that the new protection helped many industries which had hitherto found some difficulty in meeting foreign competition to secure a larger share of the home-market. Tariffs excluded or reduced foreign competition, and enabled the home-producer to raise his prices or keep them from falling, thus diminishing the consumer's margin for the purchase of other things. But this was done at the expense of the export trades, which *could* meet foreign competition. For the exclusion of foreign goods meant that the foreigner could not get British money in exchange for his goods, and therefore could not use this money (in the only way in which it *could* be used, once we were off gold) to buy British goods or to pay debts due to British subjects. The fall, or the very small improvement, in export trade, in spite of favourable circumstances, was in part due to the very cause which stimulated home industries; and what was gained on the swings was lost, and more than lost, on the roundabouts.

In a later chapter we shall examine more closely the effects of the new protectionist system. But enough has been said to cast grave doubt upon the loud and flamboyant claim that the Government's policy had brought about a great revival of British trade. It is nearer the truth to say that this policy had retarded an improvement that was due to the general revival of world-trade, to the reduction of British money to its true level, and to the boon of cheap money.

III

It would be as unjust to lay all the blame for bad trade upon the Government as to give it the credit for such small revival as took place. The real causes of bad trade, not only in Britain but all over the world, were the confusion of the world's monetary system, and the plague of economic nationalism that had spread over the globe. Britain had no doubt intensified her own difficulties by falling a victim to the plague; but the main cause of her sufferings was that all countries alike were doing their best to shut out her goods and all other imported goods.

The ruinous effects of this state of things were generally realised, even by the politicians who were busily engaged in raising fresh obstacles. In the summer of 1933, under the auspices of the League of Nations, an international economic conference was summoned in London, to discover whether some agreement could not be reached as to the means of escaping from this *impasse*; and the fact that the conference met in London, and was presided over by the British Prime Minister, threw upon the British Government the onus of taking the lead.

In preparation for the conference, a committee of experts drawn from many countries was entrusted with the task of drawing up the agenda. In putting forth the agenda, which was drafted with elaborate care, the assembled economic experts of the world issued a grave warning to the civilised peoples. They urged that unless the obstacles to international trade could be overcome, or greatly reduced, the whole economic system might break down, there might be a universal reduction of the standards of life, and this might be followed by revolutionary upheavals. In face of this warning, the delegates met with a deep sense of responsibility: the American Secretary of State, Mr. Cordell Hull, expressed a general conviction when he said: "If—which God forbid!—any nation should obstruct and wreck this great conference, with the short-sighted notion that some of its favoured local interests might temporarily profit, while thus indefinitely delaying aid for the distressed in every country, that nation would merit the execration of mankind."

Yet the conference was a complete fiasco. Its only outcome was an agreement among some of the great food-producing countries to reduce their output in the hope of raising prices: in other words, the abundance which the fruitful earth offered for the use of man was to be restricted because Governments would not allow it to reach the peoples who needed and wanted it. Who was responsible for this unhappy failure? Which of the Governments of the world merited "the execration of mankind"? America had refused to permit the discussion of war-debts; but this did not matter much, because the problem was soon to be solved by the all but universal refusal to pay these debts. America had also refused to fall in with any scheme of monetary stabilisation, because her new President was bent upon trying monetary experiments in the attempt to deal with his own economic crisis. France and the other Gold Standard countries made it clear that they would be content with no solution of the monetary problems which did not involve a general return to the Gold Standard. These unbending attitudes made it futile to attempt any scheme of monetary stabilisation.

But there still remained the great subject of trade restrictions—including not only tariffs, but the more vicious new method of "quotas," under which Governments restricted by edict the amount of this commodity or that which their people might purchase from this country or that. These restrictions were the main cause of monetary confusion; because protectionist countries, by refusing to accept from their debtors payment in goods, had set up an intolerable drain of gold, and had caused many countries, in self-defence, to enforce rigid restrictions on the movement of money. Trade restrictions were equally the cause of the unremunerative prices which were ruining the food-producing countries, and making it impossible for them to buy from the manufacturing countries. For when the food-producing countries found their products excluded by tariffs and quotas from the countries that should have been their natural customers, they were compelled to sell their goods for what they would fetch, often at a dead loss. If tariffs and quotas could be reduced all round, a long step would have been taken towards the solution of the other problems. Some countries were beginning to realise this. Holland, Belgium, and Luxemburg, for example, had reached an agreement at Ouchy for the reduction of tariffs among themselves, and were ready to admit any other country to share the agreement. Unfortunately other countries could claim, under their commercial treaties, to be admitted to these privileges without lowering their own tariffs; and unless this provision could be modified, the Ouchy agreement could not succeed. Instead of encouraging the Ouchy plan, or offering to join in it (which might have led to great results), the British Government insisted upon its rights under the "most-favoured-nation" clause, and so killed this promising experiment.

A real advance might have been achieved at the Economic Conference in the reduction of trade barriers if one of the great trading countries had been ready to give a lead; and this function ought naturally to have fallen to Britain, which is more dependent upon foreign trade than any other country. It is possible, though unlikely, that an all-round agreement for the reduction of tariffs and the abolition of quotas might have been reached. It is highly probable that experiments on the lines of the Ouchy Convention might have been encouraged by a general agreement that the "most-favoured-nation" clause in commercial treaties should be modified so as to make such experiments possible: the American countries later reached such an agreement at Monte Video. Britain might even have proposed a new group on Ouchy lines, and if she had done so, not only the Ouchy States but the Scandinavian countries and others would probably have joined, and a wide area of freer trade might have been formed, which might have grown until it had covered the greater part of the world.

But the British Government adopted a sternly negative attitude. If America and the Gold Standard countries prevented a solution of the monetary problem, it was pre-eminently Britain that prevented any advance towards a solution of the problem of trade barriers. Before the conference even met, the Chancellor of the Exchequer had foreclosed the issue by announcing that, whatever other countries might do, Britain would never abandon her tariffs. During the conference debates, Mr. Chamberlain admitted that *excessive* tariffs were harmful, but he did not attempt to indicate when they became excessive, leaving each country to settle that question for itself. Every country thinks the tariffs of other countries excessive, but regards its own as just and reasonable. The British Government made it clear that it saw no use in any attempt to lower all tariffs by agreement, and that it was opposed to any group-agreements such as Holland, Belgium, and Luxemburg had attempted at Ouchy. As for quotas, America advocated their total abolition; and it had been understood that, when the British Prime Minister visited the American President shortly before the conference met, they had agreed upon the abolition of quotas. But when the official view of the British Government was laid before the conference, it appeared that Britain was opposed to "arbitrary" quotas, but favoured "production or marketing" quotas. No attempt was made to explain the meaning of this distinction, which is, in truth, entirely meaningless; for there is no quota that the ingenuity of man could invent which would not affect the production or the marketing of the commodity to which it was applied. In short, the British Government, instead of using a great opportunity to lead the world, or a part of it, towards greater freedom of trade, offered a flat negative to every proposal that looked in this direction, and must be held primarily responsible for the breakdown of a conference upon which great hopes had been built, and for sentencing their country and the world to a continuance of insane economic nationalism, and of the suffering and impoverishment which economic nationalism causes.

The conference might have failed whatever attitude the British Government had adopted. But the attitude which it *did* adopt was an illuminating demonstration of the outlook and spirit for which it stood.

IV

The chief reason why the Government had upheld the vicious quota system at the economic conference was that it had already entered upon a policy for the revival of British agriculture which involved the application of quotas on a large scale. For this policy Mr. Walter Elliot was mainly responsible. We shall discuss it and its results in a later chapter, and no more need be said about it here. But it occupied a great deal of the attention of Parliament during the years 1933–5.

A second major subject of these years was the revision of the system of Unemployment Relief, which was a necessary consequence of the change made by the First National Government, when it took over from the Unemployment Insurance Fund the responsibility for providing for unemployed workers not strictly covered by insurance. This subject also will be dealt with in a later chapter. But it should be noted that there was unconscionable delay in working out the scheme. The first regulations were met with such an outburst of indignation that they had to be suspended, and the minister responsible for them had to be transferred to another office. The regulations had not assumed their final form when the election of 1935 took place. They were still undetermined when the proofs of this book were passed, in July 1936.

Widely as their subject-matter varied, these two measures, the new system of unemployment relief and the new system of agricultural marketing, had one feature in common: a feature which reappeared in other aspects of this Government's work. They set up nominated irresponsible bodies, to which were given large powers, unchecked by the law, over the livelihood and liberty of action of important sections of the people; and they thus involved a material invasion of popular liberty. Under the new unemployment scheme, a small board was given very extensive powers of regulating the amounts payable to unemployed persons, and the conditions on which they were to be paid. Under the Agricultural Marketing Act—a long and complicated measure which was rushed through all its stages in a single day by a docile majority—the Board of Agriculture was empowered to set up Marketing Boards for various products, with power to decide how much of each product might be grown, and at what price and to whom it might be sold; nay, more, with power to make laws binding upon all producers, to fix penalties for the breach of these laws, and to adjudge cases arising out of the laws which it had made. We shall have occasion to study these experiments more closely in a later chapter.

One wonders what has become of the liberty that English people were supposed to enjoy when one learns that it is illegal for anybody to grow hops for sale unless his name is on a Government list. Must the writer look forward to the day when he will be fined or imprisoned for publishing such a book as this, on the ground that his name is not on a Government list of approved writers—drawn up for the noble purpose of restricting the over-production of books?

It is in harmony with this general tendency of National legislation that the power of taxation has now been largely withdrawn from Parliament and entrusted to a small Commission of three members.

But perhaps the most outstanding illustration of the readiness of a National Government to invade the ordinary liberties of free men was provided by the Incitement to Sedition Bill which was introduced in 1933, and carried into law, though in a much modified form. The purpose of the Bill seems to have been to prevent the diffusion among the fighting men of the army and navy of Communist or Pacifist literature which might possibly persuade them that it is wrong to fight. We have long assumed—indeed, it is an essential element in the democratic idea—that grown men ought to be trusted to form their own opinions about the books, papers, and pamphlets which they read. Once this position is abandoned, there seems to be no logical stopping-place short of the Fascist or Nazi idea that the Government ought to prevent the whole nation from hearing or reading anything that might undermine their confidence in its wisdom. The method in which this dubious aim was to be attained was even more remarkable than the aim itself. Any magistrate was to be empowered to issue to the police a general search warrant empowering two constables to enter any house and search for literature of the kind to which the Government objected. General warrants were made illegal, as an intolerable invasion of liberty, as long ago as 1769. They were now again to be made legal, in order that a trembling Government might be armed against a wholly imaginary peril. This monstrous Bill had most of its teeth drawn, during discussions in the House of Commons, before it passed into law, and it is now a relatively harmless measure. But it is perturbing that any British Government should ever have thought of putting forward a measure such as this was in its first form. Evidently it is still true that the price of liberty is eternal vigilance. With such a blind and docile majority as the National Government controlled, even this Bill might have been rushed through all its stages in a single day, like the Agricultural Marketing Bill. Even under a parliamentary system, liberty is not safe so long as one party enjoys so unqualified a dictatorship as the Conservative Party has enjoyed since 1931.

V

In Imperial affairs, the record of the National Government was very mixed.

One great and noteworthy achievement stands to its credit in the Government of India Act: whether this measure establishes peace in India or not, it was a bold and generous enactment. More truly than any other part of the Government's work, it was genuinely "National" in character; for all the British parties, along with representatives of many schools of thought in India, shared in, and made contributions to, the long discussions which preceded the introduction of the Bill. It was not a dictated measure, nor was it imposed by the will of a single party. The only serious opposition to it came from a powerful section of the Conservative Party. It was a model for the discussion and (we may hope) the solution of a difficult and controversial question by the amicable interchange of views between men of different outlooks and backgrounds; and if other problems had been dealt with in the same temper, the National Government would have fully deserved its name. Perhaps, indeed, this very liberal treatment of the Indian problem could only have been carried successfully by a predominantly Conservative Government, like the treatment of the Irish question in 1920; for if the measure had been introduced by a Liberal or Labour Government, it is more than likely that the Conservatives would have fiercely opposed it, as they opposed the Irish Home Rule Bills and the concession of self-government to South Africa. If this is so, it forms a real compensation for the grave errors in other fields which (in the view of its critics) the National Government has committed.

There was a marked contrast between the handling of the Indian problem and the handling of the Irish problem. In Ireland, as in India, there was a fever of anti-British sentiment, which could only be allayed by tactful, temperate, and considerate handling. During the ten years of Mr. Cosgrave's government in Ireland, this fever had been substantially reduced. But it still survived. It constituted the chief political capital of Mr. de Valera, who succeeded to power in Ireland in 1932. Himself a passionate hater of England, he knew that his position was secure so long as he could make it appear that, in spite of the concession of Dominion status, England was still tyrannising over Ireland. Almost his first act was to refuse payment of the interest on the British loans whereby the Irish farmers had been enabled to purchase their farms. He had a case for withholding these payments; the British Government had a case, probably a stronger one, for claiming them. This was obviously a question which lent itself to settlement by arbitration. Mr. de Valera was willing to accept an arbitration under the League of Nations. The British Government would only agree to an arbitration by representatives of the other Dominions, on the ground that this was a domestic concern of the British Empire, with which the League had nothing to do. But it was wrong to let such a punctilio stand in the way of peace; and the manners of Mr. J. H. Thomas, the Dominions Secretary, did not make agreement easier. Heavy special duties were imposed on imports, especially of cattle, from the Irish Free State: they amounted in 1935 to £4,691,000, and were inevitably regarded by the Irish farmers as a proof of English tyranny. If the matter had stopped there, either the importation of Irish cattle would have ceased, or the British consumer would have paid the duty—that is to say, either the British Government would have got no compensation for the withheld interest, or it would have got it from the British taxpayer! But Mr. de Valera overcame this dilemma by paying subsidies to the Irish farmers to enable them to overleap the duties—that is to say, he made the Irish taxpayer shoulder the burden instead of the Irish farmer or the British taxpayer! Could there be a more grotesque illustration of the folly of tariff warfare? The only result was to embitter feeling on both sides, especially among the Irish, and to strengthen the position of Mr. de Valera.

The most important and the most discussed aspect of the Imperial policy of the Government was the Ottawa Conference—a forlorn and ineffectual attempt to turn the British Empire into a closed market. We shall discuss it fully in a later chapter. In the meanwhile, three features of these agreements deserve comment. In the first place, Britain was required by the Dominions to impose, in their interest, certain duties on foreign imports which the British Parliament had not thought to be necessary in the interest of the British people, and to pledge herself not to withdraw these duties without the consent of the Dominions. No corresponding condition was imposed upon any of the Dominions. In the second place, it was provided that all Dominion products should be admitted to Britain free of duty. No corresponding provision was made regarding the admission of British products to the Dominions. There were many who contended, when they grasped these provisions, that Britain ought to apply for Dominion status! But even more important than these remarkable provisions was the agreement that Britain should reverse her traditional policy in regard to the dependent colonies, to which she had long admitted the traders of all nations on equal terms with her own, and should compel these colonies to impose duties against foreign imports, with preferences for imports from Britain and the Dominions. The momentous importance of this departure, not only for the dependent Empire, but for the countries without colonial possessions, and consequently for the peace of the world, does not seem to have been at all realised by the negotiators at Ottawa. Even serious students of politics are only now beginning to realise its gravity.

VI

By common consent, the least successful aspect of the National Government's policy was its treatment of foreign affairs; and this was the more serious because there has seldom been a more momentous period in international relations than these four years, which saw successive challenges to the League of Nations and the collective system from Japan, Germany, and Italy; which saw, consequently, a very grave decline in the prestige and authority of the League of Nations; which saw the long and futile discussions and the unrelieved failure of the Disarmament Conference; and which saw, finally, the beginning of a new and very dangerous competition in armaments, threatening the outbreak of another ruinous world-war. How far these failures can fairly be attributed to the policy of the British Government cannot here be discussed: they will be dealt with in detail in a later chapter. It is enough here to say that Britain certainly failed to take the lead which was waiting for her in the League; and that the almost unanimous judgment of Europe regarded her as a very half-hearted and spiritless supporter of the collective system of peace.

This was the judgment also of a large and growing body of opinion in Britain. The Government was fain to recognise the force of this opinion; and evidently made a concession to it when, on the reconstruction of the ministry in June 1935, Sir John Simon was displaced from the Foreign Office. There followed an unexpected outburst of vigour; the new Foreign Secretary, Sir Samuel Hoare, electrified the world by a speech at Geneva, and Britain seemed at last to have taken the leadership of the League. On the strength of the immense increase of prestige thus acquired, the General Election of 1935 was precipitated. A month later all these hopes were betrayed.

The general survey of the work of the Second National Government which we have attempted in this chapter does not suggest a favourable verdict upon its achievements, and may seem to some readers to be biased. It is manifestly an incomplete survey, which ought to be strengthened and solidified. This will be the task of the succeeding chapters; and the reader is asked to reserve his judgment until he has followed the closer analysis of one branch of the Government's work after another which they will offer to him.

CHAPTER V

NATIONAL FINANCE

It was to avoid a collapse of our national system of finance, to balance the Budget, and to restore British credit, that the First National Government was formed. The maintenance of financial stability was therefore the primary duty of the Second National Government; and its chief claim to credit is that it is believed to have triumphantly achieved this object.

I

When, in April 1932, Mr. Chamberlain opened the first Budget of the new Government, he had first to report on the results of the work of the First National Government, and then to make provision for the needs of the coming year. The success with which the First National Government had done its work was shown by the fact that there was a surplus of £364,000, after providing £32,500,000 for repayment of National Debt; and this result was achieved without resort to protective tariffs. Mr. Chamberlain anticipated a large yield in the next year from the new tariffs which had just been imposed. He could also anticipate a large reduction of the interest payable on National Debt, as a result of the scheme for the conversion of War Loan which the First National Government had bequeathed to him; but he could not announce this publicly, since the scheme had not yet been launched. He estimated that, without making changes in taxation (other than the new tariff), he would obtain a revenue of £766,800,000 and a surplus of £800,000. These expectations were gravely disappointed. The revenue for the year 1932–3 fell short of his estimate by £22,000,000, and the expenditure exceeded his estimate by £11,000,000. This was, no doubt, mainly due to the continued decline of trade; but it was also due to the failure of the tariffs to yield the expected revenue. He also had to pay £29,000,000 for the American Debt, for which he had made no provision, though he must have known it would have to be paid. This was the consequence of Mr. Baldwin's debt settlement: in 1931 German reparations had stopped, and the payments due to us from the Allies were not forthcoming: the whole burden of the American Debt therefore had to be met without any counterbalancing payments. This left Mr. Chamberlain with a deficit of no less than £62,000,000 as compared with his estimates, and a seriously unbalanced Budget. The situation was partly helped by the reduced charges on the National Debt, due to the conversion of War Loan, which amounted, for part of the year, to £13,700,000. He also reduced the sum allotted for repayment of debt from £32½ millions to £17¼ millions, thus breaking the good record maintained by the First National Government. In this way the actual deficit was reduced to £31,000,000—not a very auspicious start!

For 1933–4 Mr. Chamberlain could anticipate great economies. He would get the full advantage of the conversion of War Loan as well as a very low rate of interest on temporary borrowings, and this gave him a reduction in expenditure of nearly £50,000,000. He proposed a new and much more modest scheme for the repayment of National Debt, which yielded him in the event a saving of nearly £25,000,000. He made no provision at all for the American Debt, but ultimately made a "token payment" of only £3,300,000, which gave him a saving (as compared with what he ought to have paid) of nearly £26,000,000. By these means—by the saving on debt interest, by the practical abandonment of the repayment of debt, and by the practical repudiation of the American debt— he made so enormous a saving that he was able to reduce the beer duty, and to make various allowances on the income-tax. Even so, he was left with a surplus of £31,000,000, which automatically went to the repayment of debt, and cancelled out the deficit of the previous year.

This more favourable situation, together with the fact that he had decided to pay nothing to America, made it possible for him to promise, for the next year (1934–5), a restoration of the cuts in unemployment pay which had been made in 1931, and of half the salary cuts made in the same year. He also reduced the income-tax by 6d., and this alone cost £20,000,000. Even so, the returns for the next year showed a surplus of £7,000,000; and by adding to this a raid on the Road Fund to the tune of £4,500,000, Mr. Chamberlain was able to promise still further reliefs for 1935–6 —the restoration of the remaining 1931 cuts in the salaries of civil servants; a reduction of the entertainment tax for lower priced seats; and sundry reliefs for the smaller payers of income-tax.

When we review the finance of these four years as a whole, the results certainly appear impressive. Most (not quite all) of the special burdens imposed to meet the crisis of 1931 had been removed, including the extra sixpence on the income-tax; and the spectacle of large annual surpluses and successive remissions of taxation did much to restore confidence in the financial stability of Britain, both at home and abroad.

How had these results been attained? The first cause was the revival of trade, from 1933 onwards, the causes of which we have already examined: the trade revival not only led to an improved return from income-tax, it greatly diminished the cost of unemployment relief, now directly assumed by the Exchequer. The second cause was the reduced cost of the National Debt, due to the conversion of War Loan and the lower rate of interest on temporary borrowings: this represented a saving of something like £50,000,000 a year. Both of these causes were healthy and sound. But the Government can scarcely take credit for the trade-revival, which was almost world-wide; and the conversion scheme would have been carried out whatever Government had been in power.

There were, however, three other causes of the budgetary improvement which were not so healthy. One was the non-payment of interest on the American Debt, which formed a bad precedent for other debtors. Another was the reduction on the provision for the repayment of National Debt. If the annual provision of £32,500,000 for this purpose (in addition to any Budget surpluses) had been maintained throughout the four years, as it had been loyally maintained by the First National Government, more than £130,000,000 would have been paid off. Mr. Chamberlain made provision for only £37,000,000 during the period; and even his surpluses (which automatically go to debt-redemption) do not materially affect this figure: for his deficit of £31,000,000 in 1933 must be set against his surpluses of £31,000,000 in 1934 and

£7,000,000 in 1935. The practical abandonment of debt-redemption was one of the worst features of the Second National Government's finance.

There is another feature of the Government's handling of the National Debt which deserves comment. While the annual charge was reduced, the capital liability was steadily increased, year by year. The total dead-weight debt (i.e. debt not balanced by assets), which had been £7,500 millions in 1929, had been reduced to £7,469 millions in 1930, and to £7,413 millions in 1931; but it began to rise again as soon as the Second National Government assumed power. It was £7,433 millions in 1932, £7,643 millions in 1933, £7,822 millions in 1934, and in 1935 fell slightly to £7,800 millions—an increase of £387 millions in four years. It may be said that only the annual debt-charge matters, and that, so long as that is reduced, it does not matter what happens to the capital. But this is a very unsound view. Some time or other, the dead-weight debt has to be paid off, or at any rate reduced; and the Government which not only makes wholly inadequate provision for paying it off, but actually adds to it at the rate of £387 millions in four years, can scarcely be commended for its handling of the nation's capital account.

II

One other feature of Mr. Chamberlain's Budgets deserves special notice. The Second National Government has been praised for effecting great reductions of taxation, and it is true, as we have seen, that it got rid of most (not all) of the special burdens which had been imposed upon the nation in 1931. But it did no more than this. And, on the other side, it imposed new tax-burdens, through its tariff system, far heavier than those it removed.

The revenue from Customs duties (i.e. taxes on imported goods), which had been only £35 millions before the war, had risen by 1930-1 to £121 millions, thanks to the incomplete system of protection embodied in the McKenna duties, the safeguarding duties, and so forth. In the following years it increased rapidly: £135 millions in 1931-2, £166 millions in 1932-3, £179 millions in 1933-4, £185 millions in 1934-5— an increase of £64 millions in four years. These duties did not cease to be taxes because they were concealed in the price of the goods on which they were imposed. Nor can it be pretended that they are paid by anybody but the purchaser: even the crudest protectionists no longer venture to suggest that "the foreigner pays." The importer, for example, of an American car pays his price to the manufacturer of the car, say, £200. He then pays, separately, the duty, say, £66 13s. 4d. He computes his own standard profit, say, 25 per cent, on his total outlay of £266 13s. 4d., and the purchaser, pays the whole sum, say, £332 13s. 4d. Sometimes, no doubt, the manufacturer reduces his price in order to be sure of his market, but he would be equally likely to do this if there were no tariffs. There is no doubt about it: the purchaser pays the duty, and its effect is either to increase the price, or to prevent it from falling.

Nor is this the end of the burden on the purchaser. It is not only the foreign import that is raised in price by the tariff. The price of the competing English product is also raised under the shelter of the tariff, though not necessarily to the same extent: this, indeed, is the very purpose for which the tariff is imposed—to secure a better price for the home-producer. It is true, as we have been loudly told, that many commodities upon which a tariff has been imposed have not risen in price, and it is argued that therefore we must assume that two and two no longer make four. The explanation is simple, and twofold. On the one hand, there have been in all countries great developments in labour-saving devices, especially in new industries such as motors and artificial silk; and these have tended to lower prices, and therefore to conceal the effects of tariffs. On the other hand, the utter disorganisation of world-trade has forced producers, especially of raw materials, to reduce their prices even below the cost of production; and this also has tended to conceal the effects of tariffs. But for tariffs, these factors would have caused a great reduction in the price of almost all commodities; the reduction has been neutralised by the tariffs, which have kept up the prices of both home and foreign products.

If, therefore, we wish to estimate the extent of the burden imposed upon the purchasing public by tariffs, we must not limit our view to the actual duties paid into the exchequer; we must take into account their effect upon the prices of home-produced goods. If the actual duties paid into the exchequer amount to £60 millions, the additional money taken from the purchasers may be as much as £120 or £180 millions, most of which will have gone, not into the exchequer for the relief of taxation, but into the pockets of British manufacturers.

A Scottish purchaser was recently trying to make a choice between two machines, one English, the other American, and both at the same price. The salesman urged him to be patriotic and "buy British."

"Wait a moment," said the Scot. "There's a duty on the American machine, isn't there?"

The salesman agreed, pointing out that this helped the English manufacturer to compete with the American.

"Well," said the Scot, "if I buy the American machine, it seems that about a quarter of what I pay will go to the British Government, and perhaps help to reduce my income-tax. But if I buy the English machine, the money will go into the private pocket of an Englishman. That's right, isn't it? Hang it all, I *will* be patriotic, as you say. I'll buy the American machine *and help to balance the Budget!*"

This heavy burden of new taxation—twice or three times as great as the £64 millions that actually comes to the exchequer—falls with the heaviest weight upon the poor, for nearly all articles of common consumption are now taxed. In effect, the poor are taxed for the benefit of the well-to-do. One of the greatest reforms of the last century was the progressive transfer of the burden of taxation from the mass of the people to those most able to bear it, by the progressive substitution of direct for indirect taxation. This process is now beginning to be reversed.

III

The annual Budget statements, which we have hitherto been considering, tell us nothing about some of the most important aspects of the Government's financial policy.

It was deeply concerned to maintain the value of

the pound sterling and "to prevent further depreciation of the currency." But what exactly did this mean? Was it the object of the Government to maintain the value of the pound in relation to gold, or in relation to the other principal currencies of the world? Or was it to secure that the purchasing power of the pound should remain steady in Britain? It was soon made clear that—except as a distant objective—the Government had abandoned the idea of fixing the pound to gold, either on the old basis or on some new one. There was, in fact, a substantial depreciation of the value of the pound in gold, or (to put the same thing in another way) a considerable increase of the price of gold in British money—one result of which was to bring out large quantities of hoarded gold, especially in India: the large influx of gold into Britain, which we shall have to consider in the next chapter, was partly due to this. The main object of the Government was to maintain the value of the pound in regard to things in general, that is to say, its purchasing power: to make sure, if possible, that prices in Britain did not go up or fluctuate sharply. This could largely be achieved by managing the issue of money, which was the work of the Bank of England. But at the same time they were anxious to prevent violent fluctuations in the relations between British and other currencies. Once the pound was no longer anchored to gold, there was apt to be a rise in the value of British money if the foreign demand for pounds was larger than the British demand for other currencies, and vice versa. To prevent or check these fluctuations, a very large fund, known as the Exchange Equalisation Fund, was formed, and was very secretly administered by the Bank of England and the Treasury, who bought or sold foreign currencies as seemed necessary. On the whole this system was well managed; and the steadiness of the value of British money compared very favourably with the fluctuations of the moneys of other countries. Thanks mainly to the Bank of England and the Treasury officials, this was one of the most successful achievements of the Government. But it was due to skilled financial management. Protectionist policy had nothing to do with it.

A second and even more important aspect of the Government's financial policy was the control which it exercised over the use of capital. The banks were stuffed with money which they could not use in the ordinary way for loans and advances to industry, because trade was so stagnant that there was no outlet for it. It might have seemed that in these circumstances the Government and the financial authorities would have been eager to get all this frozen money out, and into use; but this was not their view. There were two ways in which it might have been used, while opportunities for profitable investment continued to be lacking in Britain. One was in loans to or investments in foreign countries: half the world had always looked to Britain for loans of this sort to carry out development work; and when such a loan was made it usually involved, directly or indirectly, the production and export from Britain of capital goods for development work. The other way in which idle money might have been employed was by raising Government loans to carry out works of national development at home: this sort of policy, which had long been advocated by Mr. Lloyd George and many others, would have brought about a substantial reduction of unemployment, and would thereby have greatly reduced the expenditure on unemployment relief; while it would at the same time have permanently improved the equipment of the country. But the Government sternly set its face against both of these methods of bringing about trade activity.

At first, perhaps, there was a special reason for this policy. The great conversion of War Loan was in prospect. If the holders of War Loan had seen alternative outlets for their money, they might not have been so ready to accept a reduced rate of interest, but might have claimed repayment in cash, re-investing it in foreign loans or in Government development loans at home. The success of the Conversion scheme was, indeed, largely due to the absence of alternative modes of investment; in other words, it was made possible largely by the deliberate maintenance of trade stagnation.

But when the conversion was successfully achieved, in the summer of 1932, the justification for this rigid attitude largely disappeared. Yet the practical (though unofficial) embargo on the issue of foreign loans was still maintained. Perhaps the reason was that it had become very difficult to get payment from the countries to which the loans would largely have been made. But the main reason for this difficulty was that trade in these countries also was stagnant, and loans for useful and productive purposes would have helped them to revive. Indeed, the policy of the Government in regard to debtor countries pursued a vicious circle, and is very difficult to comprehend. First, by means of tariff restrictions, they made it difficult for the debtor countries to meet their obligations by sending goods. That set up a drain of gold, and almost forced these countries to impose exchange restrictions in self-defence or to default in their payments. Then they declared that, since these countries were not paying their debts, further loans to them must not be made, and thus the only way of bringing about trade revival and fostering British exports was precluded.

The Government's attitude towards works of national development at home was equally rigid and equally short-sighted. There were multitudes of things that needed to be done, and would have to be done sooner or later; they could be done most cheaply when money was idle and could be got at a low rate of interest, and when labour was idle and had to be maintained at great cost to the community. The Government simply would not listen to argument on this point. At the World Economic Conference of 1933 America urged that all countries should agree to undertake schemes of public works as the best way (short of the removal of trade barriers, which nobody would consider) of bringing about trade revival; and several other countries pressed the same view. But the British Government set its face rigidly against any such projects. We shall have to discuss this question more fully when we come to deal with the Government's treatment of unemployment; here it is considered only as an aspect of their financial policy.

It would seem, in short, that the Government's only devices for restoring prosperity to the country and ending the ruinous stagnation in world trade were (1) to keep the value of British money steady—a sound aim, in which they were successful; (2) to impose artificial restrictions on the movement of trade, a policy with which we shall be concerned in the next chapter; and (3) to keep money cheap, that is, to make it possible for business men to borrow at a low rate of interest, to enable Government itself to raise temporary money very cheaply, and to let municipal bodies and trading concerns replace their fixed-rate obligations at a lower rate. Now, so far as it goes, cheap money is no doubt beneficial to industry. But money is only very cheap—its owners are only ready to lend it at a very low rate—when the outlets for it are insufficient. To keep money cheap by stopping up the outlets through which it might have flowed into fruitful trade activity was surely a very left-handed way of encouraging trade revival.

Taken as a whole, then, the financial policy of the Second National Government was short-sighted and unimaginative, and showed nothing of the grasp and vision that were needed in these difficult times.

CHAPTER VI

UNEMPLOYMENT POLICY

THE average of unemployment during the four years of the Second National Government has been higher than the average of any other four years in British history. It is right, therefore, that this Government should be judged by the spirit in which it approached this terrible problem.

There is no doubt as to the cause of the widespread unemployment from which we have suffered. It is due to the catastrophic decline of our world-trade. When we were prosperous, about one-third of our total production was sold abroad, and therefore about one-third of our working population, say, 3,500,000, were engaged either in producing goods for export, or in the transport and marketing of these goods. When the volume of our overseas trade was halved, one-half of these workers were necessarily deprived of employment; and the fact that their spending power was seriously diminished involved a further large increase in the number of the unemployed even in the home trades. This is the explanation of our army of 2,000,000 unemployed workers.

The blame for this state of things cannot be wholly, or perhaps even mainly, put upon the Government: it was due mainly to the plague of economic nationalism which is ruining the whole world. But it cannot be denied that the Government has intensified this evil, by itself adopting the policy of economic nationalism. The main object of its policy has been to prevent us from buying goods from abroad, and consequently to prevent us from sending out goods to pay for them. Beyond a doubt, this policy has greatly intensified the sufferings of the export trades and of the districts in which they are mainly carried on; and any increase that has been brought about in the activities of the home trades is far more than balanced by the decrease in the export trades. The unemployment figures are sufficient proof of this.

Nor has the Government made any serious attempt to allay the plague of economic nationalism throughout the world. It had an opportunity of taking the lead in this respect in the Economic Conference of 1933, and many nations would have followed a bold lead. But it threw this opportunity away. It preferred to limit itself to bilateral trade treaties, the complete futility of which is demonstrated in another chapter of this book.

The National Government, then, has made no attempt whatsoever to grapple with the fundamental causes of unemployment, but has rather intensified them. What has it done (*a*) in regard to the relief of unemployment, and (*b*) in the provision of useful work for the unemployed? To answer these questions is the purpose of this chapter.

I

The cost of unemployment relief was one of the chief causes of the financial crisis of 1931. Even in 1930 the situation was so serious that the Labour Government appointed a Royal Commission to go into the matter. At that date those workers who were properly insured, i.e. who had paid at least thirty weekly contributions into the Unemployment Fund during the two previous years, were entitled to draw "standard benefit" for as long as seventy-four weeks if they fell out of work. But others who were not properly insured—who might have paid no more than eight contributions during the two previous years—were paid what was called "transitional" benefit at the same standard rates. The result of this was that the Unemployment Fund had become insolvent, because it was being used, without the consent of the contributors, for purposes for which it was never designed. Except in 1923 and 1924, its income had never equalled its expenditure in any single year since 1920; and in the middle of 1931 the accumulated debt on the Fund amounted to £86 millions, and was increasing by a million a week. The fact that we were *borrowing* money at such an enormous rate to provide relief for the unemployed was one of the chief reasons why confidence in British financial stability was shaken.

The Commission of 1930 recommended that the period of benefit for insured workers should be reduced from seventy-four weeks to twenty-six; that the contributions should be increased; that the benefits should be reduced; that, in the case of "transitional" benefit (though not in the case of insured workers), there should be a "needs test" before benefit was paid; and that certain anomalies, such as the drawing of benefit by married women whose husbands were in full work, should be abolished. The Labour Government carried an "Anomalies Act" to deal with this difficulty; and, when the crisis became acute, it was ready to establish a "means test" for uninsured workers, though it subsequently repudiated this proposal. But it did not tackle the other proposals of the Royal Commission. Its general attitude was, and seems still to be, that all unemployed persons, whether insured or not, should receive the standard rate of benefit without regard to their needs or resources.

The First National Government had to deal with the unsound financial condition of the system. It transferred to the Exchequer the responsibility for "transitional" benefit paid to uninsured workers. But it still left the accumulated debt as a burden on the Fund, though this was due to an improper extension of the Fund for which the State was responsible, and which the State ought to have met. It reduced the standard rate of benefit by 10 *per cent*, and increased the contributions payable by employers, workers, and the State, the largest increase being imposed upon the workers. In spite of this increase, it reduced the period for which the insured worker might draw benefit from seventy-four to twenty-six weeks. This general worsening of the insured worker's position was due to the necessity of enabling the Fund to meet the accumulated debt, which (since it was due to State action) the State ought to have taken over and added to the National Debt. Finally, the First National Government established a Means Test for uninsured workers; the means of beneficiaries, and the deductions to be made on this account, were to be assessed by the Public Assistance Committee, which meant that this type of unemployment relief was to be associated, as never before, with the system of Poor Relief. But it was clear that the new method of relieving the uninsured unemployed, and the basis on which the Means Test was to be administered, would have to be worked out in detail. This task the First National Government was unable to undertake. The crude working of the scheme under the Public Assistance Committees produced such variations between district and district, and in many cases such hardships, that a special Act had to be passed in 1932 to provide that disabled unemployed men should not be penalised by counting the full amount of their disability pensions or Workmen's Compensation allowances as forming part of their normal incomes, and by saving them from being forced to sell or mortgage the houses some of them had bought in happier days.

Two years passed before the Second National Government introduced the Unemployment Act of 1933, which tried to put the new system on a sound basis. This Act made provision both in regard to the insured workers and the recipients of "transitional" benefit. So far as the former were concerned, a longer period of benefit was allowed to those who had paid their contributions regularly for five full years. But the Insurance Fund was still left to bear the burden of the accumulated debt, and the unduly high premiums were left undisturbed. The old rates of benefit were, however, restored in 1934; this was part of the restoration of the "cuts" of 1931.

It was, however, the system of relief for uninsured workers which formed the chief feature of this Act. A special Unemployment Assistance Board of seven members was set up, with very large powers, to administer the system. It was to have full authority to regulate the allowances to be made to all uninsured unemployed workers; and in fixing their allowances, it was required to take account of the needs of the recipient and his dependents, and the resources not merely of the recipient, but *of all members of the household*. It was obvious that this might cause many quite indefensible hardships, and many attempts were made during the discussions on the Bill to secure safeguards against these possible evils; but the huge majority of the Government defeated these attempts. The new Board was only required to report to Parliament once a year. This meant that the whole body of uninsured unemployed would be left at the mercy of an almost irresponsible body, and that even Parliament would have no right to interfere for the "redress of grievances."

Two years had passed before the Government was ready to propose its new scheme, though it might have been worked out in a month. Another year passed before the Regulations under the Act, drawn up by the Board, were reported to Parliament—the Regulations which were to determine, in particular, the conditions under which family incomes were to be computed for the purposes of relief. These Regulations were rushed through in December 1934. But as soon as their effects were realised in the country, there was an almost universal outburst of indignation. Some authorities simply refused to apply them, and went on paying allowances on the old basis, unsatisfactory as that had been. It was evident that the "household means test," whereby the incomes of sons and daughters preparing to take up house on their own account were lumped with those of their parents, and whereby thrift was penalised and family relations were strained, would be quite unworkable. Members of Parliament, even Conservatives, returning from their constituencies, reported that these Regulations simply could not be enforced. They had to be suspended, and a temporary Act, which in effect allowed the previous scales of relief to be continued, had to be hurriedly passed. The Minister of Labour had to be transferred to another office; and a new Minister had to be appointed to undertake the difficult job of coming to an agreement with the irresponsible Board. This was in February 1935. In July 1936 the new Regulations were still not forthcoming.

This is indeed a pitiful record of procrastination and inefficiency in dealing with a subject of urgent importance. The Second National Government had taken four and a half years to consider a subject that ought to have been dealt with in three months; and even then it had reached no conclusion. Its handling of the Means Test had aroused deep resentment. It was entirely just that some test of his resources should be imposed before an unemployed worker was paid, at the cost of the community, allowances to which he was not entitled by any contributions which he had made. When a man owned houses that brought him an annual income of £250, it was manifestly wrong that he should receive (as happened in one case) a weekly allowance of 23s. 8d. from public funds. But while it was right that the applicant's income from other sources than his job should be taken into account, it was wrong that the incomes of his whole household should be computed as if they were his own. A just settlement of the Means Test ought not to have been difficult. It need not have taken so long as four and a half years.

II

In the provision of useful work for unemployed workers, the Second National Government was as unsuccessful as in the organisation of a just system of relief.

Here were 2,000,000 workers standing idle, and supported by public funds. Their strength, their skill, their energy were among the nation's primary assets.

With every week of idleness, strength, skill, and energy declined. There can be nothing more disheartening or enervating than the sense that society has no use for a man. On every ground, human and economic, it was of primary importance that this cruel wastage should be stopped, or at least reduced to a minimum. Was there no useful work that would add to the efficiency and amenity of the country, upon which these men could be employed, earning wages in self-respect instead of living on doles? Were there no roads to be made, no waste-lands to be redeemed, no water-logged lands to be drained, no slums to be cleared, no ports to be improved, no canals to be deepened, no water-power to be developed, no forests to be planted, nothing to be done in the resettlement of the land? There were multitudes of such tasks waiting to be undertaken, which would increase the country's efficiency, and which could be pressed on when trade was slack, and slowed down when trade revived; and these tasks could be most economically undertaken at a time when every man employed upon them represented a saving in unemployment relief. A programme of this sort of course involves large capital expenditure. Was there no money available? The banks were clogged with idle money, for which its owners could find no use, and which they would be glad to lend to the Government at a low rate of interest. But if this money was borrowed for the purposes described, there would be an annual interest charge, perhaps as heavy as the annual subsidy for beet-sugar! This frightened the Government, who could not believe that there would be adequate compensation in the increase of the nation's resources, in the savings on the dole, and in the preservation of the strength, skill, and energy of thousands of workers.

A policy of national development of this kind would not, it is true, provide a *cure* for unemployment; nothing could do that short of a restoration of international trade, which the Government made no serious attempt to bring about. But such a policy would at least provide an alleviation of a great evil, pending the return of better times. Public Works of the kind described had been undertaken on a great scale, and with a large degree of success, in several countries—in France, in Italy, and in America; and at the World Economic Conference of 1933 it had been strongly urged that the general adoption of these methods would give a stimulus to trade revival. The British Government gave a stony negative to these proposals.

In Britain there were many advocates of such a policy; bankers and economists and great industrialists joined in urging it. The chief protagonist of the cause was Mr. Lloyd George, backed by the whole Liberal Party (with the exception, of course, of those who had linked themselves with the Government). Mr. Lloyd George had been urging this policy with immense vigour since 1929. In 1934 he started a public agitation on the subject. In the spring of 1935 he laid detailed proposals before the Government, and held a series of discussions with members of the Cabinet. The Government turned down his proposals. Thereupon he published them (July 1935); and the Government promptly issued a reply under the title of "A Better Way to Better Times," in which it was argued, first that these proposals were impracticable and wasteful, and secondly that they were already being carried out. The "Better Way," it was urged, was to go on with the

Government's existing policy, and to do nothing in particular for the diminution of unemployment. Yet the Chancellor of the Exchequer had predicted that on that basis abnormal unemployment was likely to continue for ten years.

III

There was, however, one aspect of the unemployment problem to which the National Government was compelled, reluctantly and tardily, to give some attention. This was the case of what came to be known as the Distressed Areas, or (employing a convenient euphemism which the Government preferred) the Special Areas.

These regions—Durham and Northumberland, South Wales, West Cumberland, and parts of Scotland, to which parts of Lancashire ought to have been added—had, until recently, been the greatest wealth-producing areas of the country, because they were the homes of the great export trades, especially coal, cotton, shipping, and shipbuilding. They had been brought to ruin by the world's economic nationalism, and by the Government's own protectionist policy: it was largely at their expense that some other parts of the country were enjoying a mild and insecure prosperity. In these limited areas a very high proportion of the total volume of unemployment was to be found; at least 25 per cent, and in some districts 50 or 100 per cent of the working population had lost their means of livelihood, and lived miserably and without hope on unemployment pay and poor relief. It was only after the introduction of the Government's protectionist policy that they came to be identified as *par excellence* the distressed areas.

One would have thought that the dreadful plight of these once prosperous regions would have weighed continually upon the minds of the country's rulers. The first serious discussion of this problem took place in the House of Commons in July 1932. *A year later* it was announced that the Government thought of voting £500,000 for the needs of the distressed areas: this sum may be compared with the lavish subsidies voted for the handful of farmers who grew sugar-beet. *Nine months later* four Special Commissioners were appointed, one for each of the scheduled areas, to visit these regions of misery and make proposals as to what could be done to help them. The reports of the Commissioners, which made painful reading, were published in November 1934, when the Government had been in power for three years. They contained many useful proposals—mostly drawn from the schemes advocated by Mr. Lloyd George and other supporters of a policy of National Development. The Government did not think of carrying these proposals into effect. In its leisurely way it appointed two further Commissioners, one for England and Wales, and the other for Scotland, to study the question further; and voted the princely sum of £2,000,000—about a quarter of the cost of a single battleship—on which the Commissioners were to be allowed to draw for schemes to alleviate the distress of many millions of British subjects.

In July 1935 the first report of the Commissioner for England and Wales, Mr. Malcolm Stewart, was published. It contained, in moderate but unmistakable terms, an implicit indictment of the Government's policy and methods. The Commissioner pointed out that he was restricted even in the use of the very modest sum assigned to him, by limitations imposed by the Government. For example, if he proposed to make a grant to a local authority in an impoverished region to carry out some needed work that would give employment, he found that he was precluded from doing so if the service concerned were one to which Government grants could be made: in such a case he could do nothing, even if no Government grants were being made by the Department concerned!

The Commissioner strongly urged that the problem of the distressed areas could not be effectively dealt with in isolation. He put in a forcible plea for a policy of national development, such as Mr. Lloyd George and others had vainly urged upon the Government. "It is difficult to assume," he wrote, "that nothing can be made available for spending on national works. . . . Is there not to-day a need for the creation of national physical assets to replace those inherited from the past, many of which are becoming obsolete? . . . Is not their replacement in many cases overdue, and if undertaken with vision, could not we assist the expansion of industry, which would bring increased general prosperity, and decrease unemployment?"

If the "vision" which the Commissioner saw to be necessary had been available, idle labour and idle capital, instead of running to waste, could have been used to increase the health and improve the equipment of the country. But the vision was lacking; and "where there is no vision, the people perish."

Such is the record of the Second National Government in regard to the cruel problem of unemployment, which their policy had done much to intensify. For cold timidity and lack of imaginative sympathy, it is surpassed only by their record in foreign affairs.

CHAPTER VII

THE EFFECTS OF PROTECTIONIST POLICY

THE principal achievement of the Second National Government was the introduction of a system of Protection in Britain; and it is claimed that the modest improvement in trade which has taken place during the last three years has been due to this policy. We have seen, in an earlier chapter, that this improvement can be fully accounted for by three factors which were quite independent of the tariff system—a general increase in world trade which was shared by many countries, and by some more fully than by Britain; our departure from the Gold Standard, which had over-valued British money and handicapped the export trades; and the low rates of interest which followed the great conversion of War Loan. But it is necessary to examine more closely the claims put forward on behalf of the protectionist policy.

In introducing the new tariff system at the beginning of 1932, the Chancellor of the Exchequer set forth a list of seven advantages which he hoped would accrue from the new system. These were as follows:

(1) The rectification of the adverse balance of trade.
(2) The raising of additional revenue.
(3) The prevention of further currency depreciation.
(4) The transfer of employment to this country from the countries that had previously sent us their goods.
(5) The encouragement of industrial efficiency.
(6) The acquisition of a means of bargaining with

other countries for the reduction of their tariffs against us.

(7) The establishment of a system of reciprocal trade within the British Empire.

It will be convenient to deal with these claims in the order here given. No. 2 and No. 3 have, however, already been discussed in Chapter V, and No. 7 deserves a chapter to itself. The remaining four arguments will concern us in this chapter.

At the outset, however, it should be noted that some of these claims are mutually destructive. Revenue can only be raised by tariffs if the foreign goods come in and taxes are paid upon them; but employment can only be created if the foreign goods are kept out by the tariffs. The use of tariffs for bargaining implies that our tariffs will be reduced or abolished in return for a corresponding reduction or abolition of foreign tariffs; and in so far as this result is achieved, we shall have to do without the revenue that would otherwise be paid on these imported goods, and without the additional employment that their production at home is supposed to yield. If tariffs really do yield the advantages promised, why should we forgo these advantages in order to reduce the tariffs of other countries, which are presumably yielding the same advantages to them? Shall we not be reducing the prosperity of both sides to the bargain? It seems unreasonable to claim that all these incompatible advantages can be reaped at the same time.

I. *The Balance of Trade*

Before we can profitably discuss this subject, it is necessary to be clear as to what we mean by "the

Balance of Trade"; for a great deal of nonsense has been spoken and written about it.

According to the crude view which many people still hold, a country has a "favourable balance of trade" when its exports exceed its imports, that is to say, when it gives more than it gets. It has an "adverse balance of trade" when its imports exceed its exports, that is, when it gets more than it gives. This queer theory is a relic of the days when it was supposed that the chief object of foreign trade was to get as much gold and silver as possible; an "adverse balance" was supposed to drain gold and silver out of the country to pay for our imports, while a "favourable balance" was supposed to bring gold and silver into the country to pay for our excess of exports. This was really nonsense; the movements of gold and silver were always small. If you look at the trade returns for the generation before the war, you will find that our imports were always much larger than our exports; yet our gold was not drained away, but, on the contrary, tended slightly to increase.

The reason for this is that a large proportion of our imports do not need to be paid for by exports. Some of them come to us as interest on our investments in other countries; others as payments for the services of our ships, which do a large proportion of the carrying trade of the world; others again as payment for various banking and insurance services which are rendered by British financiers to the traders of all countries; while yet others represent the value of remittances sent by British subjects abroad for the support of their families at home. All these and other minor items have to be set off against our excess of imports before a true balance can be struck. They are commonly described as our "invisible exports."

But it is extremely difficult to make a true balance; and although the Board of Trade does its best, and each year makes an estimate of the Balance of Trade for the previous year, this cannot be much more than a guess, though it is a useful guide.

Even the figures for imports and exports, though carefully compiled, cannot be wholly trusted. If you compare the official figures for British exports to France (or any other country) with the French official figures for British imports into France, you will find that the French figures are always much higher, though you would expect them to be exactly the same. The reasons for this discrepancy are two. In the first place, the value of imports always includes the cost of freight and insurance, which is not included in the value assigned to exports. In the second place, imports are, broadly speaking, valued at their selling price in the country to which they are sent, while exports are in many cases valued at what they cost the exporter, which may be a very different figure. How misleading it may be to compare the value of exports with that of imports, and to assume that if the imports are more valuable than the exports the difference will have to be somehow made up, may be illustrated by a simple example. A British merchant buys £5,000 worth of goods and sends them out to be sold by his agent (say) in West Africa: that is put down as "exports £5,000." The agent sells the goods at a handsome profit, and then lays out the money in buying, let us say, ivory and palm-oil, which he sends to England: when they arrive these goods are valued at £10,000, and the entry is made "Imports £10,000." In the eyes of common sense, Britain has made a profit of £5,000, having got that much more than she gave. But according to the theory of Balance of Trade, this transaction has created an adverse balance of £5,000—Imports £10,000, Exports £5,000—which will somehow have to be made up! Evidently the calculation of the Balance of Trade is a very tricky business, which may easily lead us astray.

This is still more evident when we try to calculate the value of what are called the "invisible exports." Take, first, the interest on our foreign investments. These, in the main, represent what may be called deferred payments for exports sent out long ago. A British Company, for example, has provided the cost of building a railway in the Argentine; it has sent out vast quantities of steel rails and locomotives made by British labour; and it gets its return when the railway begins to pay, in the form of interest. But the interest has to be paid to the British shareholders in British money; and the only way in which this can be done is that wheat and meat and other Argentine products should be sent to Britain and there sold for British money wherewith to pay the shareholders. If we make it difficult (by tariffs or otherwise) for the Argentine goods to be sold in Britain, we shall be making it difficult for British shareholders to get their interest.

In this sort of way Britain has, during the last century, invested vast sums of money in developing the resources of the undeveloped countries of the world, and thus increasing the world's abundance. It is estimated that these foreign investments amount to something like £4,000,000,000. But that is a suspiciously round figure. Obviously it is impossible to state with precision the value of all the investments made by British investors in all parts of the world. Nothing better than a probable guess is possible, and the experts differ as to the amount. It is equally impossible

THE EFFECTS OF PROTECTIONIST POLICY 103

to give a precise figure for the interest due, or actually paid, on these investments. If we accept the total of £4,000,000,000, interest at 5 per cent would give us something like £200,000,000 a year which ought to be coming into Britain, in the form of imports not needing to be paid for by current exports. But what the actual figure is in any year, who can tell? The Board of Trade makes a guess. But it can't be more than a guess. Thus, for the three years 1933, 1934, and 1935, the Board of Trade puts down the interest in foreign investments at, respectively, £160 millions, £175 millions, and £185 millions. Are we to conclude that our income from this source increased by exactly £15 millions between 1933 and 1934, and by exactly £10 millions between 1934 and 1935? Obviously these figures are mere guesses.

Again, who can possibly tell how much has been earned by all our ships, tramps as well as liners, plying between port and port in all the seas of the world? The Board of Trade makes a shot. It tells us that our earnings from shipping were in 1933 £65 millions, in 1934 £70 millions, and in 1935 £75 millions—that is to say, they increased by exactly £5 millions a year. Could there be a more obvious guess? It is even more difficult to make a trustworthy estimate of what has been earned by the services rendered to the traders of the world in Banking and Insurance. The Board of Trade asks us to believe that we earned exactly £30 millions in this way in each of the three years: whether the volume of trade on which these commissions were earned increased or decreased, the commissions remained exactly the same! Finally, there is no means of telling just how much we received in remittances from British subjects abroad, and from other sources, such as tourist profits. The Board of Trade asks us to believe that every year we get exactly £10 millions from these sources, which is manifestly absurd.

The plain fact is that all these guesswork figures are quite untrustworthy as a basis for calculation. The Board of Trade is not to blame for this uncertainty. But when a Government department is called upon to put down guesswork figures which are to be used as arguments for a certain policy, the temptation to make the guesses suit the policy must be pretty strong.

And there is still another, and a more serious, element of uncertainty. We know precisely how much gold and silver comes into or goes out of the country each year. Ought we to add these figures to the totals of imports and exports? Undoubtedly gold and silver are commodities, just as much as iron and copper; and when we buy gold from South Africa, we have to pay for it, as for other goods, by giving our own goods or services in exchange. For this reason the Board of Trade always included gold and silver in its returns, until the Second National Government came into office. Then the practice was suddenly changed, and gold (but not silver) was omitted altogether. The reason given was that a good deal of the gold and some of the silver sent into this country was not the property of British subjects, but was merely deposited by its foreign owners, who might withdraw it at any time. And this was, and is, undoubtedly true. But it is also true that a great deal of the gold imported and exported *was* the property of British subjects. The Board of Trade could not tell how the gold should be apportioned between British and foreign owners, so it decided to omit gold altogether. It may be true that it would be misleading to include *all* the gold in the

THE EFFECTS OF PROTECTIONIST POLICY

calculations; but it was unquestionably misleading to omit it all. For this concealed one of the results of Protection. By putting on tariffs, and making it difficult for our debtors to pay us in goods, we were setting up a drain of gold towards this country, just as France and America had earlier done. Gold was coming in instead of goods; and this ought to be shown in our annual "balance of payments."

Under Free Trade, and down to 1931, the inward or outward movements of gold were quite small. But in 1931 we had a *net export* of gold of £34 millions. How much of this was due to the withdrawal of foreign balances and how much to British payments in gold, no one can say, though probably most of it consisted of foreign balances in that year. But in each of the following years we had large net *imports* of gold: £18 millions in 1932, £191 millions in 1933, £134 millions in 1934, and £55½ millions in 1935—a total of £399 millions, or more than eleven times as much as was withdrawn in 1931! Are we to suppose that this consisted entirely of foreign-owned deposits? Is it not much more likely that it mainly represents payments from our foreign debtors, whom we were preventing from paying their dues in goods? If that is so, then to omit gold from the "balance of payments" must seriously falsify the accounts—much more seriously than to include it.

So much emphasis has been laid upon this "Balance of Trade" question that, at the risk of tedium, it seems desirable to deal with it in some detail.

During the whole Free Trade period (apart from the abnormal war years), if we set against our imports our visible and invisible exports as computed by the Board of Trade, there was always a large "favourable balance," which represented the profit on our total foreign trade. In the prosperous years before the war, this balance was usually in the neighbourhood of £200 millions a year. That huge sum was available for investment abroad; it was mainly spent on British capital goods for export, such as railway material and machinery, the production of which gave a great deal of employment; and it added year by year to the volume of our investments which helped to pay for our imports. After the war, the amount of this annual profit on foreign trade seriously declined, especially when we returned to the Gold Standard at too high a level. But it was still substantial. Even in the year 1926, when trade was disorganised by the General Strike and the Coal Strike, the estimates of the Board of Trade gave us a small "favourable balance."

The outstanding fact, then, is that under Free Trade there was always a "favourable balance," and usually a very large one, until 1931. In that one year there was an "adverse balance," and this was adduced as a reason for abandoning Free Trade. We are entitled to ask, first, whether the protectionist policy has reversed this "adverse balance" of 1931, and, secondly, whether it has given us better results than we obtained under Free Trade. For this purpose, it will be desirable to examine the figures, year by year, since 1929, giving first the balance according to the recent practice of the Board of Trade, omitting gold; and then showing how the balance would be altered by the inclusion of gold.

In 1929 we had a "favourable balance," on the Board of Trade basis, of £123 millions. But in that year we had a net *export* of gold of £15 millions, raising the "favourable balance" to £138 millions.

In 1930 the financial crisis was beginning. Our "favourable balance" was reduced to £44 millions on the Board of Trade basis. But we had a net *import* of gold of £5 millions, which reduced the "favourable balance" to £39 millions.

In 1931—still under Free Trade—we had, for the first time, an "adverse balance" on the Board of Trade basis of £104 millions. But our net *exports* of gold, £34 millions, reduced the adverse balance to £70 millions.

In 1932—the first year of Protection—we had, according to the Board of Trade, an adverse balance of £56 millions; but as we had a net *import* of gold of £18 millions, the "adverse balance," including gold, was £74 millions—worse than the crisis year.

In 1933 world-trade was beginning to mend. According to the Board of Trade, we had in this year an exact balance between imports on the one side and exports (visible and invisible) on the other. But we had a net gold *import* of £191 millions, and therefore (if gold be included) an "adverse balance" of £191 millions.

In 1934 the Board of Trade again gave us a small "adverse balance" of £2 millions; but as we had a net gold *import* of £134 millions, the "adverse balance," including gold, was £136 millions.

Finally, in 1935, the Board of Trade was able to compute that we had a "favourable balance" of £37 millions: the first since the crisis year of 1930, when the Board of Trade gave us a balance of £44 millions. In 1935, however, we had an unusual sale of £62 millions of silver to America: but for this there would have been an adverse balance. Moreover, our net *import* of gold, in 1935, was £55½ millions; so that, if gold be included, we had an "adverse balance" of £18 millions.

The result of this analysis is that, even if we disregard gold altogether, the National Government has never been able until 1935 to obtain a "favourable balance," while even in 1935 the balance was less "favourable" than in the crisis year 1930: under Free Trade, on the other hand, there was always a "favourable balance," and usually a very large one, until the crisis year 1931.

But, as we have already shown, it is quite wrong to disregard gold. No doubt the export of gold in 1931, and some of the imports of gold in later years, have been due to the movement of foreign deposits. But the great bulk of the imports of £400 millions of gold which have taken place since 1931 is certainly due to the fact that when a creditor country erects tariffs, and so makes it difficult for its debtors to pay it in goods, it sets up a drain of gold towards itself. The bulk of the gold imports of the last four years must therefore be included in the balance. And, that being so, it may safely be said that *there has been an "adverse balance" in every year of the Second National Government*; and the claim that Protection would redress "the balance of trade" is shown to be wholly without justification. The reverse is the truth. We have been deprived of the profits on foreign trade out of which in the past we made great investments abroad, to the immense advantage of our export trades. It is not surprising that protectionists are now saying very little about the Balance of Trade, on which they had so much to say in 1931.

Why has Protection had this result, unforeseen by its advocates? They thought that if we had an excess of imports, the best thing to do was to reduce the imports by tariffs. They did not see that it is impossible to shut out imports without also shutting in the exports that go to pay for them. They did not see that imports are inward cargoes for our ships, and exports outward cargoes; and that if both are cut down by the action of Government the earnings of our shipping must decline, as they have done. They did not see that if we make it difficult for our foreign debtors to pay what they owe us in goods, they must either pay us in gold (which to a considerable extent they have done), or not pay us at all (which to some extent they have also done). No doubt it is better to get gold than nothing; but there is very little satisfaction to be got out of a heap of yellow metal, as France and America have learnt. Again, they did not see that if we deliberately cut down the volume of trade there must be a decline in the profits we make from financing and insuring that trade; and this must be so even if the Board of Trade suggests that we make exactly the same amount from this source, whether trade is good or bad. In short, they did not see that a protectionist system must inevitably reduce, not only the export of goods, but, still more seriously, the "invisible exports" of shipping and financial services, and the interest on our foreign investments, whereby we have hitherto been able to pay for whatever we wanted to buy from the rest of the world; and that the result must be not to "redress the balance of trade," but to give us an "adverse balance."

So much for the first of Mr. Chamberlain's claims.

II. Protection and Unemployment

The claim most loudly made on behalf of Protection was that it would, by shutting out foreign goods, increase the amount of work available for British workers. "Tariff reform," the hoardings shouted, "means work for all." The form which Mr. Chamberlain gave to this claim was that tariffs would *transfer* employment to this country from the countries which had sent us their products. Observe that he did not claim that there would be an increase of the total amount of employment, but only that we would employ men here by putting men out of work in other countries, and thus depriving them of the purchasing power, some part of which would have been spent on British goods. Other countries are doing the same thing. They are all "transferring" employment from other countries to their own, without trying to increase the total amount of employment available for the workers of the world. They are all trying to become prosperous at one another's expense.

Has the protectionist system been successful in reducing the volume of unemployment in this country? Has the combined effect of the protectionist systems of all countries been to reduce the total volume of unemployment in the world? The second question is easily answered. The effect of universal protectionism has been to raise the total volume of unemployment in the world to the appalling figure of something like 20,000,000—twenty millions of workers starving in the midst of potential plenty because they are not allowed to exchange their own products for the abundance which the earth produces.

As for the first question, it can be tested by figures.

During the period before the war, when a complete system of Free Trade existed in Britain, the number of unemployed workers seldom rose above 500,000. During the period after the war from 1921 onwards, when an incomplete system of Protection was being developed with McKenna Duties, Safeguarding Duties, etc., the total hovered round 1,000,000, and was mostly above that figure. In 1921 it rose for a brief moment to 2,000,000, but the recovery was rapid under Free Trade: 2,038,000 at the end of 1921, the figure fell to 1,464,000 at the end of 1922, and to 1,229,000 at the end of 1923. In the financial crisis which began in the autumn of 1929 the figures rose in an alarming way: the annual average for 1930 was 1,912,000, and for 1931 2,648,000. Then Protection was introduced to provide "work for all." At the same time stricter conditions were introduced in the conditions of relief, and this had the effect of substantially reducing the number of those registered on the books of the Labour Exchanges as unemployed; but it also had the effect of driving many on to Poor Relief or Public Assistance. The figures for the following years are given below, recipients of poor relief being shown in a separate column.

Year	Average Unemployed	Poor Relief (Jan. 1)
1931	2,648,000	1,014,933
1932	2,745,000	1,143,025
1933	2,521,000	1,375,645
1934	2,159,000	1,402,725
1935	2,039,000	1,472,891

These figures show that whereas there had been a rapid recovery after the crisis of 1921, the year after the crisis of 1931—the first year of full Protection—showed an increase in unemployment of 97,000 and an increase in poor relief of 128,000. In the second year of Protection there was a decrease in unemployment of 224,000, but this was balanced by an increase in poor relief of 232,000. In 1934 unemployment went down by 362,000, and poor relief went up by 27,000. This was therefore the first year of real improvement. The improvement continued in 1935, when unemployment declined by 80,000, though poor relief still went up by 70,000.

In short, there *was* an improvement under Protection, but it was nothing like as rapid or as great as the improvement under imperfect Free Trade after 1921. We seem to have settled down to an average unemployment figure in the neighbourhood of 2,000,000. There is nothing to boast about in such figures.

Should the improvement (such as it is) be attributed to the working of Protection? It was due, on the contrary, to facts which were entirely independent of Protection: to the results of our departure from the Gold Standard; to cheap money; and to a general if slight revival of trade in the greater part of the world. Perhaps it was still more due to the "building boom" which was growing during these years; and this was certainly not due to Protection, for we have never imported any houses from abroad. In 1931 £63 millions were spent on buildings of which plans were passed by the local authorities; in 1932 £66 millions; in 1933 £83 millions; in 1934 £95 millions; in 1935 £114 millions. The more we examine the figures, the more pitiful appears the degree of improvement brought about during the protectionist years, and the less it appears possible to attribute the improvement to Protection.

A form of argument about the relations between Protection and employment which has been very popular among protectionists runs as follows: If we exchange £1,000,000 worth of American motor cars for £1,000,000 worth of British cotton goods, one set of workmen are employed in America, and another set in Britain. But if, by means of tariffs, we compel British cotton goods to be exchanged for British motor cars, then both sets of workmen are employed in Britain. This is the sort of argument which Mr. Chamberlain had in mind when he talked about "transferring" employment from other countries to this country. There would be something in the argument if we could assume that £1,000,000 more of British cotton goods would be bought in Britain if we abstained from purchasing £1,000,000 worth of American cars. But we cannot assume this, because the plain fact is that the British cotton industry already supplies practically all the needs of the British purchaser, whether we buy American cars or not, and in addition sells about two-thirds of its production abroad. The only result of the change, therefore, would be that £1,000,000 more of employment would be given to workers in the British motor-industry, and £1,000,000 less in the British cotton-industry. The "transfer of employment" of which Mr. Chamberlain speaks is not a transfer from other countries to this country, but a transfer from one British industry to another: a transfer of employment from the export trades, which were able to compete on equal terms with other countries, to the trades which could not compete, even in the home market, without Protection.

The greatest of all the export trades is still the cotton trade, in spite of its tribulations since the war. It could not be protected, because the main part of its product had to be sold abroad. It suffered from the protectionist system in two ways. On the one hand, it had to pay more for its requirements: its dyes and countless other materials, down to such things as its wrapping paper, and the bobbins on which its yarn was wound, were raised in price; and these things are important in an industry which works on the narrowest margins of profit. On the other hand, it suffered from the fact that the reduction of imports necessarily involved the reduction of exports. When a foreigner sells goods in England, he is paid in British money. But British money is of no use to him in his own country. He must therefore exchange his British money for the money of his own country with some compatriot who wants British money. But the only purposes for which he can want it is either to pay debts which he owes in Britain, or to invest it in Britain, or to buy British goods. Therefore, whenever we exclude foreign imports by tariffs, we are preventing foreigners from paying debts due in Britain, or from investing money in Britain, or (most of all) from buying British goods. It is the export trades, whose products are sold all over the world, that suffer most in this way; and the worst sufferer is the cotton trade, because it is the greatest of all the export trades, and the most dependent upon foreign markets. The effects of Protection upon the cotton industry may be seen from a few figures. In 1929 there were 554,000 workers in the cotton industry, and 479,000 of them were at work. In 1932 there were 517,000 workers, and 350,000 of them were at work. In 1935 there were 442,000 workers, and 344,000 of them were at work. The grim story of decline represented by these figures is, no doubt, mainly due to the protectionist mania of the whole world; but these results have been intensified and deepened by the protectionist policy of our own country. This is also true of the other export trades, notably coal, and of shipping and shipbuilding. It is at the expense of these trades that the protected home trades have enjoyed their modest prosperity. The "transfer of employment" which Mr. Chamberlain hoped tariffs would bring about has not been a transfer from other countries, but a transfer from the great staple trades of this country to the less efficient trades which could not meet competition on equal terms.

The protectionist theory that imports, especially of manufactured goods, deprive our own people of employment, however plausible it may appear to the unthinking, is in fact in violent conflict with the facts; because it overlooks the fact that imports have to be paid for, and can only be paid for by British goods and services. The more foreign goods we buy, the harder we have to work to pay for them. That is why, over a long series of years, the trade figures show that an increase of imports of manufactured goods does not cause an increase of unemployment, as the protectionist theory implies, it causes a decrease. Unemployment goes down when manufactured imports go up, and up when manufactured imports go down. This could be demonstrated, if need be, by the figures for fifty years or more. But it is enough to consider a few post-war figures. In 1920 the imports of manufactured goods reached the high figure of £460 millions, and in that year only 2 per cent of the employed population were out of work. In the next year manufactured imports suddenly slumped to £240 millions, and unemployment rose to 15 per cent. Between 1922 and

1929 manufactured imports rose gradually (with set-backs) to £330 millions; unemployment gradually (with set-backs) fell from 15 to 10 per cent. There was a slump in manufactured imports between 1929 and 1932—they fell from £330 millions to £160 millions: in the same years unemployment rose from 10 per cent to 22 per cent. Between 1932 and 1935, in spite of tariffs, imports slowly rose again to £185 millions; and unemployment slowly fell to 14 per cent.

In face of these figures, which refer solely to manufactured goods, it is impossible to maintain that the importation of foreign manufactures causes unemployment, or that the deliberate restriction of such imports can reduce unemployment. The very opposite is true. The more imports we receive, the more exports we shall have to send out to pay for them; the more work there will be for our ships; the greater will be the demand for financial and other services; and the greater will be the number of workers who will be employed in these ways. This is not a mere statement of theory. It is the irrefutable testimony of the facts. Far from being a cure for unemployment, Protection is a cause of unemployment; and it is because the whole world has adopted this system that there are to-day 20,000,000 unemployed workers in the civilised countries, at a time when, but for these barriers, there might be a universal diffusion of prosperity.

The disastrous effects of Protection upon employment in the export trades are poignantly displayed in the dreadful plight of the parts of the country in which the great export trades had their principal seats, and which were not long ago the wealthiest and most productive regions of Britain. Durham and Northumberland, South Wales, parts of Lancashire, and parts of Scotland, have become almost derelict areas, in which whole communities are deprived of their means of livelihood and reduced to stony despair. These districts were already suffering before the financial crisis began. But they have suffered most acutely since Protection was introduced and their foreign customers were more or less barred out. It is only under the Second National Government that they have had to be scheduled as Distressed Areas. Since their sufferings are largely due to the policy pursued by the Government, it is but right that they should receive assistance from the Government. After long delay, they were offered a sum of £2,000,000—a mere fraction of what the same Government thought it right to spend in encouraging a handful of farmers to grow sugar in competition with the tropical sun. The terrible unemployment of these regions has certainly not been relieved, but has on the contrary been largely caused, by Protection. Again, the cotton industry is to be compelled to suppress its "redundant mills," none of which would be redundant if the flow of world-trade could be restored. This is to cost £2,000,000, but the Government which lavishes subsidies upon other industries, does not even think of finding this modest sum for the greatest of all our industries. The burden is to be borne by the other mills, already struggling to keep down their costs (which the Government's tariffs have increased) in order to maintain their trade.

"Tariff reform means work for all" has been shown to be the most monstrous falsehood that has ever disfigured the hoardings. So much for Mr. Chamberlain's second main argument for the protectionist system.

III. Protection and Efficiency

One of the most remarkable of the claims made by Mr. Chamberlain was that Protection would promote industrial efficiency; for on the surface it would appear likely to produce the opposite effect, by persuading manufacturers that they could go on in their old ways behind the shelter of a tariff.

It is unquestionably true that there has been, since the war, a remarkable improvement in the efficiency of many British industries, through the development of labour-saving machinery and better organisation. But what was the motive for the energy in trying experiments which led to this improvement? Beyond doubt, it was the keenness of competition for the dwindling markets of the world. It was open competition with the whole world that kept British manufacturers on the alert.

A striking example of this was provided in the boot trade in the years before the war. English boot manufacturers had, under Free Trade, the great advantage of being able to obtain all their requirements at the lowest world price, whereas their American and other competitors were handicapped by having their costs increased by duties. In spite of this there was, for a year or two, a considerable invasion of the British market by American boots. The reason for this was that the Americans had produced very clever machines, which turned out boots more cheaply and in a greater variety of shapes and sizes. The British bootmakers clamoured for Protection, to save them from this competition. If they had got it, they would have gone on in their old ways. They were refused it; and consequently were driven to imitate the American methods.

As soon as they did this, their great advantage in getting their materials at the lowest prices became effective. In a short time "American" boots were being manufactured in Britain, and were actually being imported in large quantities into America, in spite of the American tariff. In this case—and it was a typical case—it was Free Trade that stimulated efficiency; whereas Protection would have discouraged it.

On what grounds could the advocates of Protection expect that this natural tendency would be reversed? Their chief argument was that the industries which needed reorganisation must have a secure market at home before they dare undertake the risk and cost of large reconstructions. With a secure home market, they would be able to obtain a full output; their overhead charges would then be reduced; and they would be able to undersell all competitors. If those who used this argument were convinced of its truth, one wonders why they did not at once go on to full production, and thus undersell all their competitors, while retaining the Free Trade advantage of getting all their requirements at the lowest price. But perhaps what they meant was that, if they were given a monopoly of the home market, they would be able to charge higher prices at home, and thus make the home consumer pay the cost of selling abroad at a lower price. This is what is happening in the iron and steel industry among others.

The theory that a tariff will give a profitable security to the existing manufacturers has, however, been refuted in more than one instance: expectations of big profits under the shelter of a tariff may encourage the rise of many concerns between which there may be a ruinous cut-throat competition. This happened when, before the full protectionist system was introduced, special protection was given to the new artificial silk industry. The Chairman of Courtaulds, the greatest of the artificial silk concerns, explained to his shareholders in 1931 that the unsatisfactory condition to which the industry had been reduced was due to the creation of a large number of concerns brought into existence by the prospect of earning large profits behind the tariff wall, and these were ruining the market.

When competition becomes ruinously severe there is a strong temptation to create gigantic monopolies, able to fix their own prices. This becomes practicable when foreign competition is excluded by a tariff. The growth of monopolies, trusts, combines, and price-fixing rings has been very rapid under Protection: it has, indeed, been directly encouraged by the Government. But monopoly does not necessarily imply efficiency. A monopoly may be exposed to the temptation of buying up and suppressing valuable new processes in order to avoid the trouble and expense of revising its methods. Monopoly is the child of Protection.

The industry in regard to which the argument that Protection encourages efficiency has been most freely used has been the Iron and Steel Industry. Nobody has ever suggested that the Cotton Industry or the Coal Industry could be made more efficient by Protection. But it was recognised that the section of the Iron and Steel Industry which produced crude iron and steel badly needed reorganisation in order to secure the advantages and economies of large-scale production. The Iron and Steel Industry, however, has a great many sections, and the finished product of one section is the raw material of another. The higher or more developed sections needed to get their raw materials at the lowest price, and for that reason often bought foreign iron or steel; sometimes also they wanted types of steel not produced in Britain—such as steel made by the Bessemer process. The relative importance of different sections of the industry has been indicated as follows: The production of 1,500 tons of steel bars will employ three hundred men for a week. The rolling of these 1,500 tons into tinplates will employ 1,440 men for a week. The manufacture of these tinplates into finished articles will employ 13,500 men for a week. If these figures are even approximately correct, it would manifestly be the height of folly, in order to protect the employment of the three hundred, to raise the price of steel bars to such an extent as to endanger the employment of the 14,940 other workers for whom first the bars and then the tinplates are raw materials.

Not only do the cruder branches of the Iron and Steel Industry produce the raw materials for the higher branches. The industry as a whole also produces the raw materials for many other industries of the highest importance: engineering, the motor trade, the constructional trades, among others. In fact, Iron and Steel is more nearly the basic industry upon which others rest, than any other. To give protection to it, and especially to its cruder branches, was a very risky experiment, which could only be justified by a conviction that prices would not be raised, and that the industry would be made more efficient under the shelter of tariffs on foreign iron and steel. On these grounds there was much opposition to the setting up of a tariff on Iron and Steel. Thus the Iron, Steel, Tinplate, and Metal Merchants section of the London Chamber of Commerce predicted that if the price of steel was raised, and foreign steel was excluded, Britain would eventually lose her immense trade in corrugated iron in all parts of the world. To a large extent this anticipation is being justified.

Nevertheless, a duty of 33⅓ per cent was imposed in 1932 on imports of iron and steel, for the express purpose of bringing about a reorganisation of the industry: the Tariff Commission insisted that the continuance of the duty would be conditional upon the carrying out of reorganisation, and the duty was to be withdrawn in 1934 unless an approved scheme had by that date been adopted. In January 1933 the Chairman of the Tariff Commission vigorously scolded the leaders of the industry for having done nothing. A few weeks later they produced a plan for a national body from which the chief users of steel were excluded, and which Mr. Chamberlain—no unfriendly critic— described as "a plan for establishing the machinery whereby reorganisation *may* be carried out, rather than the scheme itself." In June the head of one of the great steel concerns announced that a duty of 33⅓ per cent was quite inadequate, because foreign steel was still coming in, and that no reorganisation was possible until the duty had been greatly increased. In October it was stated that a proposed new works could not be started unless a pledge was given that Protection would be continued for twenty years. In November the President of the Board of Trade informed the industry that the Government had "no intention whatever" of withdrawing the duty. He thus made the threats of the Tariff Commission of no avail, and deprived them of their only means of enforcing reorganisation. In February 1934 the Federation of Iron and Steel Manufacturers decided to postpone reorganisation *sine die*. In May the Tariff Commission surrendered, and recommended that the iron and steel duties should be continued indefinitely; in June the Commission tamely recommended that the duties should be increased. In short, the iron and steel magnates had been bluffing all the time. They had got the duties they wanted, which put the users of iron and steel at their mercy; and they evidently had no intention of carrying out the promised reorganisation. That is how Protection encourages efficiency.

Meanwhile the users of steel were protesting without avail. The Chairman of the Metal Trades Association protested that the only result of the tariff had been to raise the price of the raw material for tinplates from £5 to £8 a ton, and that in consequence Britain had lost to Italy the whole trade in tinplates for the Spanish tinning trade. Sir John Hunter, the great constructional engineer, bitterly criticised the steel manufacturers, and stated that but for the chance of getting foreign steel the business of his concerns would have gone to the Continent. Sir Herbert Austin, the motor magnate, who had long been a strong advocate of all-round Protection, declared that "if, behind the tariff wall, rings are formed to reduce competition and keep up prices, our change in fiscal policy will be the beginning of the end of British industry." His chief rival, Lord Nuffield (Sir William Morris), also protested vehemently against the use of tariffs to raise the price of his principal raw material, and declared that if he were younger he would start making his own steel.

The Iron and Steel Industry is the one case in which

a definite attempt has been made to use Protection as a means of increasing efficiency. It has been used as a means of increasing prices, and crippling all the steel-using trades, without any real increase of efficiency. So much for Mr. Chamberlain's prediction that one of the results of Protection would be "the encouragement of industrial efficiency."

IV. Tariffs for Bargaining

The argument which had more influence than any other in bringing about the acceptance of the protectionist system even by many who had hitherto been loyal to Free Trade was the suggestion that tariffs could be used as a means of bargaining to bring down the tariffs of other countries. All over the world tariffs against British goods were growing, and it seemed that Britain had no means of retaliation. Why should foreign traders be allowed free access to British markets when the access of British traders to foreign markets was narrowly restricted? Was it not right that the admission of the traders of any country to the British market should be made conditional upon the admission of the British trader to that country's market? But no such bargain was possible until Britain had a tariff wherewith to bargain. This justification for the creation of a tariff was so plausible that, in face of the growing tariffs all over the world, it seemed irresistible.

Yet as recently as 1929 the most authoritative committee ever set up to consider the problems of British trade and industry (the Balfour Committee on Trade and Industry) had in its final report convincingly argued that these hopes were groundless.

"The tariff bargaining process," the Commission reported, "cannot in the long run lead, and as a matter of historical fact has not led, to a reduction of the general run of tariffs. The tendency is in the opposite direction, and this for a very good reason. . . . Tariff bargaining as a method of endeavouring to obtain freer access to foreign markets is only possible if the actual negotiation is preceded by the raising of the tariff on one or both sides for the express purpose of giving a margin for bargaining. Even then, the object is frequently defeated by the growth of vested interests in the interval, which refuse to allow the intended reductions to be made. The final result of the whole process is more often than not a rise instead of a fall of the tariff levels which were actually in force before the first step towards tariff bargaining was taken."

The Report went on to deprecate strongly the adoption of such methods in the hope of improving British trade. The authors of this warning could not, and did not, anticipate that their advice was so soon to be flouted, and a great experiment in tariff-bargaining so soon to be undertaken. We must examine whether the results of the Second National Government's experiments were such as to justify the hopes of the protectionists, or the warnings of the Balfour Committee. In spite of the conclusions of the committee over which he presided, Sir Arthur Balfour was at first in favour of the tariff system, on the ground that the foreigner had to be taught a lesson. But he held that this was the only possible justification for protection. "Unless the tariffs we are putting on result, by negotiations and bargaining, in an all-round reduction of tariffs," he wrote in January 1933, "they will have failed; since this country, as a great creditor country, cannot live on a high tariff policy."

The first result of the imposition of tariffs in Britain was that, within three months, twenty countries greatly increased their duties on British goods, or by means of "quotas" greatly reduced the amount of various British commodities, particularly coal, which were permitted to enter their ports. In some cases this was done for the purpose of having something to bargain with. "When visiting Belgium recently," said Sir Kenneth Lee (head of one of the greatest cotton firms) in 1932, "I found the duties on certain of our goods had been almost doubled. I asked why, and was told that when we put on our tariff they increased theirs so as to have something to bargain with." A hundred examples of this sort of thing might be quoted. We found ourselves involved in a trade war with France, which had heavily reduced the import of British coal. The war ended with an agreement in June 1934, which was hailed as a triumph for the bargaining power of tariffs; but all that the agreement did was to reduce the restrictions on British trade to the level at which they had stood before the British tariff was imposed, except in the case of coal, the quota for which was more unfavourable than it had been in 1931!

The systematic use of tariffs for bargaining did not seriously begin until after the conclusion of the Ottawa Agreements in 1932, which will be discussed in a later chapter. Then the President of the Board of Trade began "bi-lateral" negotiations with a number of countries, and boasts were made of the number of countries that were eager to conclude agreements. With immense pains, agreements were concluded with sixteen countries between May 1933 and February 1936. Great difficulties were experienced in reaching these agreements. One difficulty arose out of the "most-favoured-nation" clause in commercial treaties, which (in most cases) bound both parties to the agreements to concede to practically all countries, without getting anything in return, the advantages they gave to one another. This difficulty was evaded or overcome partly by confining the concessions to articles which did not enter into general trade, and partly by the mischievous method of fixing "quotas" instead of reducing tariffs—for example, by insisting that the other party to the bargain should take a fixed proportion of its coal from Britain, in return for Britain's taking a fixed proportion of some other commodity. Another difficulty arose from the "vested interests" to which the Balfour Committee referred: protected trades in Britain clamorously demanding that *their* tariffs should not be used for bargaining purposes. The consequence was that, for the most part, the results of these much advertised agreements were of trivial importance.

The results of the policy of bargaining by means of tariffs can best be illustrated by comparing our trade with the agreement countries and the non-agreement countries as it was in 1931 and in 1935. Here are the figures:—

	Exports.		Imports.	
	1931.	1935.	1931.	1935.
Agreement countries	£109 m.	£110 m.	£331 m.	£231 m.
Non-agreement countries	£110 m.	£111 m.	£282 m.	£240 m.

These figures bring out several striking facts. They

show that almost exactly half of our export trade with foreign countries went to the agreement countries both before and after the agreements were made. They show that the improvement in both cases has been negligible—less than 1 per cent; and that there was no greater improvement in the agreement-countries than in the others! Evidently the agreements were of no use at all, so far as exports were concerned: our export trade to foreign countries was practically no better in 1935 than it was in the crisis year, 1931. On the import side the figures are still more striking. Our imports from the non-agreement countries have gone down by £42 millions; but our imports from the agreement countries have gone down by £100 millions. Before the agreements were made, the countries which made them had a bigger trade with us than the countries which did not make them; now their trade with us is smaller. The net result of all these elaborate and loudly advertised negotiations is that they have done us no good, and they have done serious harm to the countries which we inveigled into making agreements with us.

In March 1935, after the policy of making bargaining agreements had been in force for two years, the effect of this policy upon the obstacles to our trade with other countries was summarised by the President of the Board of Trade, in answers to questions in the House of Commons. He stated (1) that changes in import *quotas* affecting British goods had been made since January 1934 in a large number of countries, of which he enumerated fifteen; and he added that "the general tendency of the changes made abroad has been to reduce imports from this country." He also stated (2) that since 1934 important alterations in *tariffs* affecting British goods had been made in a large number of countries; and he added that "in most cases the general changes were in an upward direction."

It will be observed that these statements refer only to the quotas and duties imposed since January 1934, when the agreements were being made. They do not refer to the numerous quotas and duties imposed against British trade in 1932 and 1933, as an immediate response to the British tariff policy. There is no suggestion that any of these had been reduced as a result of tariff bargaining. And it is clear that, far from having pulled down hostile tariffs from their 1931 level, our tariffs have led to an all-round increase of the obstacles to our trade; the hopes of the protectionists have been completely nullified and the anticipations of the Balfour Committee fully justified.

Such are the results of "tariffs for bargaining."

We have now examined six of the seven claims which were put forward in justification of the protectionist policy of the Second National Government, testing them by the facts and figures of four years. And here are the results:—

(1) Until 1931, under Free Trade, we always had a favourable trade balance. Since 1931 we have never had a favourable balance. The trade balance has not been rectified, but has been made worse.

(2) Additional revenue has undoubtedly been raised, but at great cost to the nation; for consumers have had to pay twice or thrice as much as the Exchequer has received from these taxes.

(3) The value of the pound sterling has been kept fairly steady—not in relation to gold, but in relation

to things in general. But this has not been a consequence of Protection. It has been brought about by the Exchange Equalisation Fund.

(4) Unemployment reached its highest level after the protectionist system had been in operation for a year. Since then there has been some improvement, though the figure is far higher than it used to be under Free Trade. Such as it is, the improvement is due to causes quite independent of Protection, which has in fact retarded it. Such "transfer of unemployment" as has taken place has not been from other countries to this country, but from the export trades to the favoured home trades; and the dreadful plight of the "distressed areas" is largely due to our protectionist policy.

(5) Protection has failed to bring about an increase of industrial efficiency, notably in the flagrant case of the Iron and Steel trade.

(6) The use of tariffs for bargaining has been a total and abject failure. The tariffs against British goods are much higher than they were before our tariffs were imposed; and this has been largely due to retaliation against our tariffs.

CHAPTER VIII

AGRICULTURAL POLICY

THE greatest constructive effort of the Second National Government in the economic sphere was an attempt to bring about a revival of British agriculture, which, like agriculture in many other countries, had been very seriously affected by the world-wide economic crises, and by the excessively low level of prices—often below the cost of production—which it brought about. The main cause of these low prices was the insanity of economic nationalism. Eager to be self-sufficient in the production of foodstuffs, many populous countries imposed high tariffs on the import of foodstuffs, in order to increase the area under cultivation. The results were twofold: in the first place, the standard of life in these countries was gravely reduced by the rise of prices, and their citizens were left with an insufficient margin for the purchase of their other requirements; in the second place, the great producing countries, excluded from their natural markets, found themselves with huge surplus stocks, which were in some cases deliberately destroyed, and in others sold at a ruinous loss. These low price-levels brought ruin to farmers all over the world, and to British farmers among the rest.

In these circumstances it was reasonable that the Government should come to the aid of the agricultural community, in order to save the land from going out of cultivation. But any emergency measures for this purpose ought to have been designed as emergency measures. They ought not to have been of such a kind as to reduce agriculture to a parasitic condition, unable to maintain itself on its own resources. They ought to have been planned in relation to the permanent conditions of British farming, and to have looked forward to a reorganisation which would have accepted, and made the best of, these conditions.

There are certain governing factors, not sufficiently regarded hitherto, which ought to be taken into account in any intelligent plan for the revival of British agriculture; and it is fair to judge the agricultural policy of the Second National Government by the extent to which it recognised these factors.

The first of them is that Britain cannot, in any event, produce more than about half of the food requirements of her crowded population. It is therefore merely futile to adopt measures which might—even if economically unsound—be in some degree defensible in the case of a country capable of being self-sufficient in regard to foodstuffs. A policy looking towards self-sufficiency is, in the case of Britain, scarcely sane.

The second is that the soil and climate of Britain are particularly well adapted for the production of just those foodstuffs which are best eaten fresh, such as meat, milk, eggs, vegetables, and fruit, and for which her great towns afford admirable markets close at hand. They are not so well adapted for the production of other important foodstuffs, such as sugar and (except in a few districts) wheat. These commodities are mostly not perishable; they can be stored for long periods, and brought without damage from the remotest parts of the earth. It would therefore appear that a sane policy would concentrate upon the first of these two groups, and be content to draw the second from other lands.

The third factor is that a majority of the population of Britain is under-nourished; and, as science has demonstrated, its malnutrition is due mainly to under-consumption of milk, eggs, vegetables, and fruit—the very things for which the soil and climate of the country are best adapted, and in which, owing to the nearness of markets, it has a great advantage over all foreign competition. What is needed to rectify this malnutrition is an abundant and cheap supply of these home-grown products.

The fourth factor is that, if the farmer is to produce these products cheaply, he must be able to obtain all his requirements—his machinery and implements, his fertilisers, the feeding-stuffs for his livestock—at the lowest possible prices. He must also be assured of getting his fair share of what is paid over the shop-counter for his products: as things are, he gets only about one-third of what the consumer pays, which seems to leave too large an allowance for the transport, sale, and wastage even of perishable articles.

The fifth factor is that the agricultural community forms only 7 per cent of the whole population, and of this 7 per cent a large majority consists of agricultural labourers, the worst-paid, and perhaps the most variously skilled, of working folk. It is right that the farmers, and still more the labourers, should be able to obtain a reasonable livelihood. But they ought to obtain it, not by raising the cost of living for the 93 per cent whom they help to feed, but by producing efficiently and abundantly the foodstuffs which these consumers most need.

The policy adopted by the Second National Government for the development of agriculture disregarded and defied all these factors. Instead of concentrating upon the agricultural products for which the soil and climate of the country are best fitted, they gave the greatest and the most costly assistance to precisely those crops for which this country is least suited—sugar and wheat. Instead of doing everything possible to cheapen, and therefore stimulate the consumption of, milk, eggs, vegetables, and fruits, which a sound nutrition policy demands, they deliberately set themselves to raise the price of these products, with the inevitable result of diminishing consumption. Instead of trying to secure that the farmer should get his requirements at the lowest possible price, they put duties upon these things, thus enhancing their price. Instead of striving to diminish the gap between the consumer's price and the producer's price, they increased it. Instead of pursuing abundance, they pursued restriction. Instead of helping the agricultural labourer, their policy resulted in a worsening of his condition.

It was impossible to resort to the panacea of tariffs in dealing with agriculture, because the Ottawa Agreements (which will be discussed in the next chapter) had given a guarantee of freedom from tariffs to the Dominions, which were and are the chief competitors of the British farmer. The methods adopted were therefore (1) the granting of subsidies, paid either by the taxpayer or the consumer; (2) the fixing of quotas for the restriction of imports; (3) the fixation of minimum (not maximum) prices for various commodities; (4) the organisation of marketing; and (5) the limitation of output.

A direct subsidy from the Exchequer was given for sugar-beet. This was an inheritance from the Conservative Government of 1924–9, which had promised the subsidy for ten years, in the hope that by that time the sugar-beet industry would be self-supporting. At the end of the ten-year period a committee was appointed to report upon the system. The committee gave a scathing condemnation of the subsidy, and urged that it should be brought to an end; nevertheless it has been continued, though its form is to be changed. Naturally it was a very costly business to put the English farmer into a position to compete with the tropical sun in the production of sugar. In effect, the taxpayer was called upon to pay for each pound of sugar produced as much as the consumer paid over the counter; in other words, British sugar cost twice as much to produce as imported sugar, and the taxpayer paid the difference. Some extra employment was thus obtained; but it would have been much cheaper to pay all the extra workers full wages to remain idle, and to give the farmers £1,000,000 a year *not* to produce sugar-beet. In addition to the large sums wasted in direct subsidies, we lost the duties that would have been paid on the displaced imports of sugar; we seriously crippled the sugar-growing British colonies; we lost the export-trade that would have gone to pay for the imported sugar; and we deprived our shipping of both-way cargoes estimated to amount to £300,000 *per annum*. The sugar-beet subsidy put some money into the pockets of a few English farmers; but most of the taxpayer's money went to the owners of the refining factories, largely foreign-owned, which could only give employment that would otherwise have been given in the ordinary sugar-refining factories.

The wheat-subsidy was given in a more subtle way, at the expense, not of the taxpayer, but of the consumer. Farmers were guaranteed a minimum price of 42s. per each quarter of "millable" wheat. The market price of wheat was (say) 25s. or less (in 1935 it sank to 21s.), and some scientific farmers, using mechanised methods, have been able to grow wheat profitably at 26s. or thereabouts. The grower sold his wheat to a miller, at the market-price, and received a certificate that he had done so; the certificate was then sent in, and the Treasury paid the extra 17s. per quarter, or whatever the sum might be. This system not only brought about an increase of 500,000 acres in the area devoted to wheat, mostly on land that might have been more advantageously used; it also lent itself to wholesale fraud. Farmers who grew wheat for poultry-food or other purposes (say, for seed), sold it to the miller and got a certificate; then repurchased it, perhaps at a shilling advance so as to share the profits of the fraud with the miller; and obtained their 17s. or more from the Exchequer. Many a dignified personage who would have been very severe upon a half-starved unemployed man taking unfair advantage of the unemployment dole, did not hesitate to defraud the community in this way by taking unfair advantage of the wheat-dole. The cost of this subsidy was met by a levy upon every sack of flour, whether milled at home or abroad, amounting at first to 2s. 6d., then to 3s. 6d., and finally to 4s. 6d. a sack. This involved a rise in the price of the quartern loaf of bread of at least ½d., and often a penny. It fell especially upon the poorest people, who have to spend a larger proportion of their income upon bread than other people. This form of subsidy, which falls upon the consumer without his realising that he is paying it, is regarded as such a masterpiece of ingenuity that it has already been extended to meat, and the Minister of Agriculture promises that it will be more widely employed.

The second method of helping agriculture is the *quota*, which is especially useful where our supplies largely depend upon imports. It affords a method of raising prices by creating an artificial scarcity. The outstanding example of this method is afforded by the case of bacon. Before the Government fixed its benevolent eye upon this popular article of diet, British people were consuming 13,000,000 cwt. of bacon, more than half of which—excellent in quality—came from Denmark. In its wisdom, the Government decided that we should only be allowed to consume 11,000,000 cwt., and that the amounts to be supplied by Danish and other importers should be severely restricted, so as to give a chance to the British farmer, who has hitherto been reluctant to produce the right sort of pigs. The artificial restriction of supplies of course brought about —as it was intended to do—a rapid rise in price; with the result that we had to pay a great deal more money to the Danes for a great deal less bacon. It is needless to trace all the confusions which resulted from this scheme. Enough to say that it increased the price of bacon to such an extent as almost to exclude it from the dietary of the poor.

The third method, that of fixing minimum prices, is best exemplified in the case of milk, in which there is practically no foreign competition. A series of marketing boards was established in all parts of the country, with power to fix a minimum price below which milk could not legally be sold, on pain of severe penalties. The increased prices thus promised encouraged the farmers to increase their production; but the rise of prices necessarily led to a fall in consumption, and many poor people had to reduce their supply, or fall back upon tinned milk. Enlarged supply and decreased consumption created a surplus. Part of this was got rid of by supplying milk free, or very cheap, to school children; this cost the taxpayer £5 millions. But most of the surplus was sold to manufacturing concerns—to the manufacturers of tinned milk, cheese, chocolate, etc.—at prices far below those at which the poorest people were permitted to buy fresh milk: the manufacturer got his milk at 6d. a gallon; the housewife had to pay 6d. or 7d. a quart. To cover the difference, the milk producers were compelled to pay a levy out of the prices that had been promised to them. Farmers were fined up to £50 for selling some of their surplus milk to poor people at less than the fixed price; and then had to see their surplus sold to manufacturers at very much lower prices, and to pay the difference in the form of a levy. Many small milk producers were driven out of business by these arrangements. But at least employment was found for a large number of officials. The effects of the scheme upon the dietary of the poor were, however, highly important; instead of increasing, it diminished the popular consumption of milk. On the other hand, it doubtless enriched some of the large producers, and enabled the big distributing concerns to make handsome profits.

The milk scheme was part of a great plan for improved marketing, and a well-devised plan for this purpose might have yielded excellent results. The Agricultural Marketing Act, under which all these schemes were put into operation, was an elaborate and complicated measure which conferred dangerously large powers upon irresponsible bodies appointed by the Ministry of Agriculture. These bodies made regulations which imposed severe restrictions upon the freedom of action of many farmers and others; and then, acting as judges in their own cause, imposed severe penalties for breaches of their regulations. One judge pointedly compared these methods to those of the Star Chamber. This Act, as the Minister of Agriculture boasted, was carried through all its stages in Parliament in a single day, with the consequence that Parliament had no time to study, understand, or amend it.

The kind of mischief which this hasty and ill-considered legislation might produce was well illustrated by some of the proceedings of the Potato Marketing Board. Influenced, no doubt, by the big potato salesmen who were represented upon it, this Board decided that in order to get a systematic plan it was necessary to get rid of the multiplicity of small salesmen, and to allow nobody to sell potatoes without a licence from the Board. Now in some districts where small holdings were numerous, the growers were only able to produce small parcels of potatoes, with which the big salesmen could not be bothered: they preferred to buy wholesale and to sell wholesale. To meet the needs of the small growers, a class of small salesmen had grown up, who went round with their own lorries, bought the potatoes from the growers, and then sold them to the greengrocers in the nearest towns—thus rendering a service to the growers, the shopkeepers, and the general public. Suddenly an edict of the Board announced that licences would not be granted to these small salesmen, who thus saw their livelihood destroyed by a decision made by an irresponsible body, against which there was no appeal. When the question was raised in Parliament, the Minister of Agriculture calmly stated that Parliament had now no right to interfere, having (without realising what it was doing) conferred irresponsible power upon these bodies in the Act which had been hurried through in a single day. Improved marketing is very necessary for the revival of agriculture, and no doubt some improvements have been brought about under the Agricultural Marketing Act; but abuses of this sort are beyond toleration.

The fifth method, that of restricting production, might also be illustrated from the policy of the Potato Marketing Board, which imposes a heavy fine upon any farmer who increases his acreage under potatoes. It can also be illustrated by the method adopted for bringing prosperity to the grower of hops. No Englishman may now legally grow hops for sale unless his name is on a Government list. The list contains the names of those who were not intelligent enough to reduce their production of hops when there was a prospect of a glut.

What has been written above is by no means a complete account of the schemes which have sprung from the fertile brain of Mr. Walter Elliot. Some of these schemes have, no doubt, been of advantage to the farmer. But they are so slapdash, so ill-considered, so high-handed, and so bureaucratic in character that their defects far outweigh their merits. There are many signs of revolt against them, even among the farmers. But for the most part farmers have accepted the new schemes, because, when all is said, they have increased prices even if they have diminished consumption, and they have transferred large sums from the pockets of the taxpayers and the consumers to the pockets of the farmers, who would be more than human if they did not welcome this transfer, even if they grumble about the multiplication of officials, and the new controls that have been imposed upon them. Apart from the increase of prices, the direct subsidies which have been lavished upon the farmers at the expense either of the taxpayer or of the consumer amount to about £26 millions a year; and although these immense sums have mainly gone to limited groups of farmers and to middlemen, their fellows seem to think that it is unwise to look a gift-horse in the mouth, since there is always hope that more may be forthcoming for them.

But if the farmers feel that they have gained a good deal, what of the agricultural labourers, who form the great majority of the agricultural community? What have they got out of the £26 millions of subsidies, and the increased prices? In the Spring of 1931, according to the Board of Agriculture, the average wage of agricultural labourers throughout England and Wales was 31s. 8d. per week. Then came considerable wage-reductions during the first two years of the Second National Government. Mr. Walter Elliot got to work, and out of the £26 millions of subsidies, and the increased prices of nearly all foodstuffs, he succeeded in raising the average wage of the agricultural labourer, by the Spring of 1935, to the princely sum of 31s. 8½d.: an increase of ½d. a week as compared with 1931. This is not enough to cover the extra cost of one loaf of bread a week which has been due to the action of the Government. It is not nearly enough to cover the extra cost of the milk which the labourer ought to be providing for his children. And this increased wage has been accompanied by a substantial reduction in the number of agricultural labourers in employment, and by an increase in the number of unemployed workers. In short, agricultural labourers are definitely worse off than they were in 1931.

It cannot be said that the achievements of the National Government in the sphere of agriculture redound to their credit. They have enriched some (not all) farmers at the expense of the taxpayer and the consumer. They have done nothing at all for the agricultural labourer. They have imposed very heavy burdens upon the Exchequer, which (along with expenditure on armaments) may help to bring us back into financial insecurity. They have caused a deterioration instead of an improvement in the nutriment of the majority of the British people. And, with all this, they have not found the true path to a genuine and lasting rehabilitation of agriculture, for this can only come through a wider demand for the foodstuffs for which our soil and climate are best suited. On the contrary, they have made it appear that the interests of the farming community are in conflict with those of the nation as a whole. The system they have established cannot last, because it makes the prosperity of one small section of the community depend upon the impoverishment of the rest.

CHAPTER IX

THE OTTAWA AGREEMENTS

AMONG the glowing hopes which protectionists entertained when the new fiscal system was established in February 1932, perhaps the brightest was the hope that it would open a new era in the history of the British Empire, an era of closer unity brought about by economic bonds; for now, equipped with a tariff, Britain would be able to make some response to the preferences which the Dominion had given or offered to her.

There were some—notably Lord Beaverbrook—who hoped for the establishment of what they called Empire Free Trade: all tariff barriers within the Empire were to disappear, common tariffs were to be erected against the rest of the world, and the Empire was to become a single great economic unit, barring out the rest of the world from the enjoyment of its vast resources. This would have been to substitute for Economic Nationalism, Economic Imperialism, which would have been even more dangerous to the peace of the world. The Government did not share these large aspirations—not, perhaps, because they disapproved of Economic Imperialism, but rather because they knew that the Dominions were too much wedded to their exclusive policies to consider any such scheme for a moment.

But they seem to have hoped that, in the world-crisis, the members of the Empire might be willing to help one another by mutual concessions. And Mr. Baldwin at any rate persuaded himself that by reducing their barriers against one another's trade, the members of the Empire might set an example to the rest of the world.

I

An Imperial Conference on these matters was fixed for the summer of 1932 at Ottawa. In preparation for it, the Dominions had been provisionally exempted from the duties that were imposed upon foreigners, and allowed to retain the immense advantage of free admission to the British market; the attempt to use the new British tariffs for bargaining with foreign countries was also postponed until it should be seen what Ottawa would bring forth. Perhaps (from a bargaining point of view) the British Government might have done better to let the duties apply to the Dominions, subject only to such preferences in their favour as would correspond to the preferences they gave. In the Dominions, also, preparations had been made for the coming bout of bargaining. In Canada the duties on British goods had been enormously increased in the spring of 1932; Canada had "something to bargain with." In Australia the tariffs had already been raised to prohibitive heights for the purpose of averting financial collapse; Australia also had "something to bargain with." So, indeed, had the other Dominions. Britain alone, in spite of her rulers' belief in the value of tariffs for bargaining, had nothing to bargain with.

From the outset it was clear that the Dominions were resolved to get as much as they could, and to give as little as they could. It was never suggested, not even by the British representatives, that in return for free admission to the British market the Dominions should give free admission to their own markets to British traders.

Indeed, the Dominions were not satisfied with free admission. They insisted that Britain should impose duties upon a number of commodities which even a protectionist Parliament had not thought it wise to tax, in order that the Dominions should have an advantage over the foreigner. These commodities included wheat, maize, butter, cheese, eggs, condensed milk, honey, fruit (raw, canned, or dried), copper, lead, and zinc. In some of these cases (wheat, copper, lead, and zinc) the British delegates stipulated that they should not be sold above the world price. If it was practicable to enforce such a provision in these cases, why was it not enforced in the others? But of course it was quite impracticable: the same article cannot be sold at two different prices in the same market; the price was fixed by the price of the foreign supply; and in all these cases the cost to the British consumer was raised by the amount of the duty. But even this was not enough. The Dominions demanded (and the British plenipotentiaries agreed) that Britain should be forbidden to alter these duties for five years *without the consent of the Dominions*! The British Parliament, in other words, was to be deprived of its control over its own taxes! No corresponding stipulation was made, or even suggested, on the other side: the Dominions would have resented fiercely any such invasion of their self-governing powers. It is not surprising that the suggestion should have been made that Britain should apply for Dominion status! This is the first occasion in British history upon which Parliament's control over taxation has been subjected to an external authority.

It will be noted that meat was not included in this

list. That was because meat was to be dealt with in another way. Britain undertook to impose "quantitative restrictions," or *quotas*, on imports of foreign chilled and frozen meat. This meant that the amount of meat imported from the Argentine (by means of which debts due to Britain were paid) was to be cut down in order that the Dominions might fill the gap. The results of this were twofold. In the first place, the price of imported meat went up, as was intended, and the British consumer was mulcted again. In the second place, the sellers of meat in the Argentine, with a reduced outlet, had to sell their meat at a sacrifice. But the British consumer did not get the advantage. The big meat-dealers were enabled to buy their meat cheaper than ever, and sell it dearer than ever.

The net result of the concessions exacted from Britain was that the obstacles to trade, instead of being diminished, were greatly increased. But what of the concessions made in return by the Dominions?

To begin with, they undertook that British goods should be admitted on competitive terms, which was explained to mean that their duties should only be sufficient to raise the cost of the imported British article to the level of that of the home-produced article. On the strength of this, one of the minor British ministers (a Simonite) boasted that the Empire had in principle abandoned Protection. The very reverse was the case. The sole purpose for which foreign trade is carried on is that the cheaper products of one country may be exchanged for the cheaper products of another; if tariffs are to be used to equalise prices, the reason for foreign trade is gone, and if this principle were carried to its logical consequence, there would be no foreign trade at all. Far from having abandoned Protection, the Empire, by adopting the "compensatory" principle, had adopted it in an extreme form.

In the second place, the Dominions reduced some of their existing duties. But the tariffs which they reduced were the very high tariffs which they had recently adopted; and in scarcely any cases were the duties brought down to the level which they had reached in 1931. This may be illustrated by a few instances, selected almost at random, from the Canadian list. The table shows the level of duties first under the Dunning tariff enacted in 1929; then under the Bennett tariff, enacted in 1932, just before the Ottawa conference; and, finally, under the Ottawa agreements:

	Dunning, Per cent	Bennett, Per cent	Ottawa, Per cent
Unbleached cotton fabrics	13·7	39·7	38·6
Cotton printed piece-goods	19	48·2	46
Cotton lace curtains	19·2	40·3	40
Wool blankets	21	92	66·2
Wool piece-goods	26	55·7	54·5
Artificial silk fabrics	22	68·5	68·5
Gloves	21·5	43·6	43·6
Carpets	23	92·5	71·5
Earthenware	19·2	43·5	43·5
Boots and shoes	16·2	39·2	39·2

It is evident that these changes made little or no difference in the freeing of trade. In Australia the results were even more unsatisfactory. "This agreement" (Ottawa), said Mr. Gullett, the Australian Minister of Trade and Customs, in October 1932, "does not reduce the protective level of our Australian tariff.... It very generally *increases* the protective level against British imports." And a month later the Australian Government declared that "the Ottawa agreement contained no promise that duties against British goods would be lowered." The duties were, in fact, lowered in twenty-six cases, and increased in 440 cases.

The third "concession" made by the Dominions in return for the "concessions" they had exacted from Britain was a promise that the preferences in favour of Britain should be increased. But the increased preferences did not involve, except in a few cases, any decrease in the duties on British goods. They were given by means of increased duties on foreign goods. In other words, the duties against British goods were kept high enough to keep most of them out; they were raised to still higher levels against foreign goods, thus increasing the barriers to the flow of world trade. But even this "concession" was largely nullified, in the case of Canada, by the imposition of a special "dumping duty" of $12\frac{1}{2}$ per cent against British goods, on the top of the ordinary tariff, on the ground that the British currency had been depreciated. The effect of this, in some cases, was to give a preference to American and German goods as compared with British goods.

In short, as an experiment in tariff bargaining, the Ottawa agreements were an utter failure. Britain was forced to give a great deal, and to raise the cost of living of her people; and in return for this, she got practically nothing. As a contribution towards the lowering of the barriers to world-trade, and an example to the world, the agreements were worse than useless. They very substantially increased the barriers to world-trade, both in Britain and in the Dominions. Finally, as a means of welding the Empire into closer unity by means of trade-bonds, the agreements were positively mischievous. The trade-bonds which they created were trade-shackles. In the eighteenth century the First British Empire was broken up mainly because the American colonies believed that their trade and prosperity were being restricted in the interest of the Mother country. In the twentieth century the bonds of Empire may be strained, if not broken, because the Mother country has been given good reason to believe that she is being treated as a milch-cow by the daughter-nations.

In this sordid bargaining there was no thought of common or of mutual benefits; each party to the bargain strove to get as much, and to give as little, as possible; and the British negotiators got so much the worst of the bargain that they almost returned home without signing the agreements, and would have done so had they not talked so loudly beforehand of the great things they were going to achieve. It would have been a good thing for Britain, for the Empire, and for the world if they had refused to sign. Yet when they returned, all the commitments they had undertaken —including the pledge that the British Parliament should not be permitted to modify some of its own taxes without the consent of the Dominions—were submissively endorsed by the "rubber-stamp Parliament" which had been elected in 1931, and which—abdicating the function of criticism which is the highest duty of Parliament—held that it was its duty obediently to commend and ratify whatever the dictators might decree.

One further "concession" the Dominions made at Ottawa: they all promised to set up "impartial" tariff commissions, before which British traders who felt that they were unfairly treated could plead their case. This concession has been proved by experience to be entirely futile and derisory.

The formal agreements at Ottawa were made only with the self-governing group of Empire countries: Canada, Australia, South Africa, New Zealand, India, Newfoundland, and Southern Rhodesia. But the non-self-governing members of the Empire, in Africa and elsewhere, were included in the purview of the conference, though their only spokesman was the British Colonial Secretary. It was agreed that they should be compelled to erect tariffs against foreign countries, with preferences for Empire countries; that is to say, to create new barriers to world-trade and against their own customers, and to restrict the access of foreign countries to the vast resources of these mainly tropical lands, without regard to the needs or interests of their inhabitants. On the wider aspects of this new policy we shall presently have something to say. For the moment we are concerned with it only as a part of the plan for forcing British trade into new channels.

This was, in truth, the main object and consequence of the Ottawa system: not to increase the total volume of British trade, but to force it into new channels. That this was so is clearly brought out in the following tables, which show in outline the change in the direction of British trade between 1931 and 1935; during the last two of these four years it should be remembered that the total volume of world-trade was increasing, and that Britain was getting a share, though by no means a large share, of the increase. The Ottawa agreements did not cause trade to flow more freely between Britain and the Dominions; but they caused it to flow with far greater difficulty between Britain and foreign countries. And the result was that proportionately Empire trade increased at the expense of foreign trade.

First consider the effects of the agreements upon the two sections of the Empire, the Ottawa countries and the dependent parts of the Empire, in a period of generally expanding trade:

Year	Exports to		Imports from	
	Ottawa Countries	Other British Countries	Ottawa Countries	Other British Countries
1931	£102 m.	£68 m.	£169 m.	£76 m.
1935	£138 m.	£66 m.	£207 m.	£77 m.
Increase or decrease	+£36 m.	−£2 m.	+£36 m.	+£1 m.

It appears from this table that while both the exports to, and the imports from, the Ottawa countries showed a substantial expansion (though not more than might have been expected in a period of expanding trade), the exports to the dependent Empire showed a decline, and the imports from these lands showed only a very small increase; yet in normal conditions these new lands, which were still in process of being opened up for commerce, ought to have shown an exceptional increase. It appears that the Ottawa agreements, though beneficial to our trade with the self-governing countries of the Empire, were harmful to our trade (in spite of preferences) with the dependent parts of the Empire; they were still more harmful to the trade of these lands with the rest of the world.

The next table shows that such improvement as there was, even in this period of expanding world-trade, was mainly due to a mere transfer of trade from foreign countries to Empire countries. For purposes of comparison, and to show how the tariff period compares with the Free Trade period, we add in this table the figures for 1929:

Year	Imports from		Exports to		Re-exports to	
	Empire Countries	Foreign Countries	Empire Countries	Foreign Countries	Empire Countries	Foreign Countries
1929	358·8	861·9	324·4	404·9	23·1	86·6
1931	247·4	613·8	170·7	219·9	16·1	47·8
1935	284·8	472·1	204·3	221·4	11·0	44·3

This table shows that, since 1931, and as a result of Ottawa, our imports from the Empire have increased by £37 m., though they are still far behind what they were in 1929; but our imports from foreign countries have gone down by £140 m., since 1931, and are little more than half of what they were in 1929. On the import side our increased trade with the Empire has been far more than balanced by an immense decrease in our trade with foreign countries. The Empire now supplies 37 per cent of the diminished volume of our imports, as against 29 per cent in 1929, and 28 per cent in 1931.

On the export side our trade with the Empire has increased by £34 m., while our trade with foreign countries has only increased by £2 m., in spite of the improvement in world-trade and the much-boomed Runciman agreements; but both our Empire trade and our foreign trade are far behind what they were in 1929. The Empire now takes 48 per cent of our total exports, as against 44 per cent in 1929 and 43 per cent in 1931. In other words, the increase of our exports to the Empire is proportionately less than the increase of our imports from the Empire. That is what one would expect from the nature of the agreements, which were designed to foster imports from the Dominions rather than exports from Britain.

If we include re-exports with exports (as we ought to do) the increase in exports to the Empire is reduced to £29 m., and our exports to foreign countries show, instead of an increase, a decrease of £2 m. Here also it is apparent that the improvement of our trade with the Empire has caused a decline of our trade with foreign countries, even in a period of expanding trade. There is not much to be said for a system which produces such results.

It is now possible to sum up the effects of the Ottawa agreements upon the course of British trade.

(i) They did nothing to increase the freedom of movement of Empire trade, but rather diminished it. But they so seriously increased the trade barriers between all parts of the Empire and foreign countries that the Empire countries were able to obtain a larger share of the total shrunken volume.

(ii) They helped the Dominions to sell their goods in Britain far more than they helped Britain to sell her goods in the Dominions.

(iii) They brought the power of the British Parliament to deal freely with its own taxation under Dominion control, but imposed no corresponding restrictions upon the Dominions.

(iv) They did not "unite" the Empire by trade-bonds; they tied it up with vexatious trade-shackles, and introduced into the relations of its members a dangerous habit of mutual exploitation and recrimination, rather than of mutual aid.

(v) They restricted the trade of the dependent parts of the Empire for the presumed advantage of its dominant members.

(vi) They hampered and shackled Britain in her negotiations with foreign countries, and made it impossible for her to take the lead in a movement for the relaxation of trade-barriers.

(vii) They forced Britain to increase her tariffs, and (yet more serious) committed her to enter upon a policy of "quantitative restriction of imports," or quotas—"those new and diabolical inventions," as Sir John Simon described them (March 19, 1936), "which are doing so much now to hamper British and world-trade."

When the agreements were under discussion in the House of Commons, Mr. Baldwin, who sometimes indulges in an outburst of inconvenient candour, put the question: "What have we got out of Ottawa? I answer quite frankly, I do not know. Nobody knows." If he had waited a few years, and had still been in a mood for candour, he might have given a more definite answer. But it would have been an answer which would have reflected no credit at all upon the Government of which (though not yet the head) he was, as leader of the dominant party, by far the most powerful member.

II

We have hitherto considered Ottawa solely in regard to its effects upon trade. But it must also be considered from a loftier point of view. We must ask ourselves what were its effects upon a vexed and restless world, visibly drifting towards war and ruin.

It was already becoming clear that the greater Powers of the world were divided into two groups, the satisfied and the dissatisfied Powers, the "haves" and the "have-nots." The satisfied Powers included Britain with her enormous Empire, France with her vast and recently acquired territories in Africa and elsewhere, the United States with her illimitable resources, and Russia with her huge territory stretching from Central Europe to the Pacific. Among the smaller European States, Holland with her rich East Indian empire, and Belgium, with her great Congolese dominion, may be numbered among the satisfied Powers. Among them, the satisfied Powers owned by far the greater part of the earth's surface, most of its supply of raw materials, and most of the territories suitable for habitation by civilised peoples. Two of them, Britain and France, were faced with the prospect of a diminishing population, which would make it impossible for them to make full use of the vast territories they controlled. They (along with some of the lesser States, most of them with dwindling populations) were the main upholders of the League of Nations, which had been created to preserve the peace of the world by defending the independence and territorial integrity of all existing States; that is to say (in the accepted interpretation), by maintaining the *status quo*.

On the other side were the dissatisfied Powers—all densely populated countries, with growing populations, which were unable to maintain their peoples at a tolerable standard of life from their own resources, and which possessed few or negligible territories beyond their own borders. They could only maintain this purpose by carrying on a large foreign trade, and they found themselves debarred by all but insuperable barriers of tariffs, quotas, and exchange restrictions which had been created in all parts of the world. They needed homes for their surplus population; and they found themselves shut out by restrictions on immigration in all the most eligible regions for settlement. They needed raw materials for their industry—especially the raw materials produced in the tropical lands, which they could not produce themselves, and which (like rubber and vegetable oils) had become indispensable for modern industry; and they saw that all these territories were engrossed by the satisfied countries, and that they were being excluded from them. It was inevitable, in these circumstances, that they should decide that they must fight rather than starve. It was inevitable that they should revolt against the system of peace represented by the League of Nations, if that system was to mean merely the preservation of the *status quo*, and if it was not to be used as a means of redressing the evils of which they complained. Statesmanship ought to have foreseen that Japan, Germany, and Italy, and perhaps other States later, were bound to rebel against the existing system, and that the rebellion must become more inevitable in proportion as the system of trade-restriction and exclusive nationalism became more intense.

It is in the light of this condition of things that we must judge the policy adopted by Britain and the British Empire during the fateful years from 1931 to 1935. Britain had been, until 1931, the greatest open market in the world; the closing of this market hastened and intensified the crisis. The British Empire covered one-quarter of the land-surface of the globe, and included the best areas still available for settlement by civilised peoples, and the richest sources of tropical raw materials. At Ottawa the British Empire made it clear that instead of alleviating the distresses of the dissatisfied countries, it meant to intensify them. That decision unquestionably contributed materially to increase the growing strain which was to bring the world to a crisis. And when, in the following year, 1933, the British Government played the leading part in destroying all hope of a freer trade system, it was clear that a large share of responsibility for the troubles that were certain to follow must rest upon the British Government.

The effects of Ottawa upon the world-situation were twofold. On the one hand, the Dominions (with the concurrence of the British Government) had made it clear that while they wanted to sell their products to the rest of the world, and especially to Britain, they intended to reduce to a minimum their purchases from the rest of the world, and even from Britain, though she was to be given a somewhat favoured position in competing for a share of this minimum. The Dominions had also made it clear (but this was independently of Ottawa) that they regarded the vast and half-empty lands which they controlled as the exclusive property of the small populations already settled in them; that since many of their citizens were unemployed as a result of the policy they were pursuing, they did not propose to admit immigration even from Britain, and still more from the overcrowded and dissatisfied countries; and, finally, that they expected the League of Nations and the British fleet to protect them in the maintenance of this exclusive and dog-in-the-manger attitude.

On the other hand, the British Government was primarily responsible for the new policy whereby all foreigners, including citizens of the dissatisfied countries, were to be restricted in their access to the immense tropical Empire of Britain and its rich materials. The British Government was responsible because it alone could (and did) issue orders to the Governments of the dependent colonies and protectorates, requiring them to impose tariffs against the foreign imports and to give a preference to British and Dominion imports.

This was a momentous departure from the colonial policy which Britain had hitherto pursued; and although it was very light-heartedly undertaken, and as little criticised at the time as the passage of the Stamp Act in 1764, it may well prove to be one of the gravest decisions of the Second National Government.

Throughout the Free Trade period Britain had always given, in all territories under her control, the same freedom of access to the traders of all countries as to her own traders. This policy had proved to be very beneficial to the colonies, since it gave them greatly enlarged markets for their products: half of the cocoa produced in West Africa, for example, was purchased by America. It was, moreover, this policy which accounted for the willingness of the world to permit the enormous expansion of the already gigantic British Empire which took place as a result of the partition of Africa and other colonial territories between 1880 and 1900. The other countries all knew that if Britain annexed any territory, its resources would be available for all the traders of the world; whereas if France or any other country annexed territory, the rest of the world would be excluded by tariffs. True that British subjects had an advantage in British territories in securing contracts or concessions; but this was less important than freedom of access for trade—opportunities for purchasing necessary raw materials, and open markets for the sale of manufactured products. This British practice had been so successful that it had been adopted in 1884 (Berlin Treaty) in respect of lands in the Congo basin, and by the League of Nations in 1920 as one of the conditions to be observed in mandated territories.

The reversal of this time-honoured policy by the Second National Government did serious harm, as we have seen, to the trade of the dependent colonies. What was far more important, it had the most unhappy effects upon the international situation, and it made the position of the British Empire far less secure. It was, in effect, a notification to the dissatisfied Powers that, so far as Britain was concerned, they were to be debarred from free access to the markets and the raw materials of some of the most valuable regions of the world. Japan had no tropical colonies; Germany had been deprived, at the end of the war, of those which she had previously possessed; Italy had nothing but some strips of arid and desert land, incapable of meeting her needs.

Speaking on this subject at Geneva, in September 1935, after the damage had been done by the Government which he represented, Sir Samuel Hoare recognised the need of the dissatisfied Powers for raw materials, and promised—the promise has not been fulfilled—that this should be considered at an international conference. But he proceeded to argue, with a blindness characteristic of protectionist mentality, that there were no obstacles to the purchase of raw materials, which all colonial Powers were eager to sell. He failed to see that the dissatisfied Powers needed not only materials, but markets for their own products; and that they could not buy unless they were permitted to sell. A British merchant can buy British colonial goods with British money. A German or Italian merchant cannot buy them with German or Italian money; he must acquire British money by selling German or Italian goods for it, before he can buy. The influence of Ottawa in accelerating and intensifying the world economic crisis, which is the chief cause of the world political crisis, and of the menace of war, must not be underestimated. The narrow view of national and imperial interests which it represented was, in fact, largely the explanation of the most pitiful failure of the Second National Government—its failure in the sphere of foreign affairs—which we shall consider in the next chapter.

CHAPTER X

THE FOREIGN POLICY OF THE NATIONAL GOVERNMENT

THE life of the National Government has been a period of intense and increasing strain in international affairs, during which it has appeared that the world was rapidly drifting towards war—a war which everybody dreaded, because everybody knew that, if it came, it would probably bring universal ruin; but which the statesmen of the world seemed powerless to avert. We have to consider in this chapter whether the British Government was in any degree responsible for this condition of strain, and whether it did all that it might have done to alleviate the strain and to avert the peril.

I

The successive crises of these years were all due to the restlessness of three Great Powers: Germany, Japan, and Italy. But these three were the chief of the dissatisfied Powers, whose position we considered at the end of the last chapter. All three had dense and growing populations; all three were incapable of maintaining their populations from their own resources, and therefore needed a great foreign trade whereby they could exchange their own manufactured products for the food and materials of other countries; all three consequently suffered in an exceptional degree from the restriction of world trade which resulted from the mania of economic nationalism and high protectionism that afflicted the world in the years following 1929.

All three were therefore tempted to use force to burst the bonds that were strangling them; and for this purpose all three put themselves under the control of military dictatorships, which could organise the whole of their resources for a struggle for existence. When the period opened, none of the three owned external possessions of any importance where they could hope to find compensations for their exclusion from the markets of the world, or supplies of raw materials, or homes for their surplus populations. The troubles of these years arose from the attempts of two of these Powers, Japan and Italy, to seize territories from which they hoped to get a relief from their distresses, while the third Power, Germany, aroused the alarm of all her neighbours by arming herself, under a ruthless dictatorship, to take advantage of any opportunity that might offer.

It is evident that the plague of economic nationalism, and the erection of barriers to trade all over the world, were the primary cause of the strain and alarm of these years.

To what extent did the policy of the British Government contribute to create this dangerous situation? In the last chapter we have seen how the Ottawa agreements amounted to a notification to the dissatisfied Powers that their trade with one-quarter of the world was to be severely restricted; and, in particular, that they were to lose the free access which they had hitherto enjoyed to the vast resources of the dependent British Empire. But, apart from Ottawa, the protectionist policy of the Second National Government unquestionably contributed to intensify the difficulties of the time. It closed to the suffocated countries the one great free market that had been open to them until 1931. How rapidly and severely the trade of Germany,

FOREIGN POLICY 163

Italy, and Japan with Britain was restricted by the establishment of Protection in Britain is very clearly brought out by the following tables, which set forth the volume of British trade with these countries, first in 1929, the last year of normal trade, then in 1931, the crisis year, and finally in 1933, 1934, and 1935, the three post-Ottawa years.

BRITISH TRADE WITH GERMANY. (*In Million £*)

	1929	1931	1933	1934	1935
Imports from Germany..	68·8	64·1	29·8	30·6	30·0
Exports to Germany ..	37·0	18·4	14·8	14·0	18·9
Total trade	105·8	82·5	44·6	44·6	48·9

Here is a catastrophic decline in trade between the two countries—in imports and exports alike—a decline which must seriously have increased the difficulties of Germany. The sudden drop from £105 millions in 1929, and £82 millions even in the crisis year, to £44 millions or £48 millions, was no doubt in part due to restrictions on the German side. But the British tariffs have their share of blame.

BRITISH TRADE WITH ITALY (*In Million £*)

	1929	1931	1933	1934	1935
Imports from Italy ..	16·8	15·1	9·2	8·4	7·9
Exports to Italy	16·0	9·9	9·1	9·3	6·8
Total trade ..	32·8	25·0	18·3	17·7	14·7

This table shows a progressive decline, year by year, until the total for 1935 is less than half of that for 1929. Evidently British policy had helped to produce the distresses of Italy.

BRITISH TRADE WITH JAPAN

(*In Million £*)

	1929	1931	1933	1934	1935
Imports from Japan ..	9·1	7·3	6·2	8·0	8·3
Exports to Japan ..	13·4	6·2	4·2	3·8	4·0
Total trade ..	22·5	13·5	10·4	11·8	12·3

This table has special interest in view of the clamour about excessive and unfair competition from Japan of which we have heard so much. It shows that both our total trade with Japan and our imports from that country have actually undergone a diminution since 1929. In, and until, 1929 British exports to Japan had always been greater than imports from Japan, and the total surplus of British exports since the war was more than £100,000,000. It has only been since Protection was introduced in Britain that Japanese imports have exceeded British exports. In any case, the absurdity of the clamour about unfair competition is shown by the fact that our trade with Japan has never been more than a minute fraction of our total foreign trade, either on the import or on the export side.

It should be noted that, in all three cases, the decline continued even during the years of reviving world trade, 1933–5. The reason for this was, no doubt, that Ottawa had made it difficult for Britain to trade with foreign countries, in order that the Dominions might benefit. In any case, it is clear that the British protectionist policy did nothing to alleviate, but much to intensify, the difficulties of the dissatisfied countries, from which sprang all the unrest of these years.

II

In the autumn of 1931, when the Second National Government assumed power, danger threatened from two quarters. On the one hand, in the Far East, the Japanese occupation of Manchuria in September had offered the most formidable challenge to the whole system of the League of Nations that had yet been delivered: we shall have to deal more fully with this question later.

On the other hand, in Europe, the situation in Germany still offered a grave problem, as it had done ever since the conclusion of the Treaty of Versailles in 1919. Under that treaty the strongest nation in Western Europe was treated as a pariah nation. The democratic Government established in Germany after the war, which had been weakened gravely by the necessity of submitting to the humiliating terms of the treaty, had nevertheless made up its mind to accept the situation and to make the best of it. It had obtained membership of the League of Nations in 1926, and, under the leadership of Stresemann, and later of Brüning, had striven, for a time successfully, to play its part in the new system of peace. It had gained something from this policy: the Rhine provinces had been evacuated by the allied armies of occupation; and the crushing burden of reparations had been first reduced by the Dawes settlement of 1924, then revised by the Young scheme of 1930, and finally brought in effect to an end by the Lausanne agreement of June 1931. But this final concession had only been made possible by the desperate financial and economic plight to which Germany had been reduced. She was still on the verge of bankruptcy; even her commercial creditors had been compelled not to press their claims for fear of collapse; the standard of living of the German people had been forced down; faced by the tariffs and quotas of the rest of the world, she was unable to export her products in sufficient quantities; and there seemed to be no outlet and no hope for her army of unemployed workers.

Moreover, she was still treated as a pariah nation. Her rich Rhineland provinces, though now freed of foreign troops, were still demilitarised, and lay defenceless before the formidable French fortresses of the frontier. She was still forbidden to possess a navy on the scale of those of the other Powers; she was still compulsorily disarmed in the midst of neighbours all armed to the teeth. No steps had yet been taken to fulfil the solemn pledges given to her twelve years earlier at Versailles that her compulsory disarmament would be followed by the voluntary disarmament of other Powers. A Disarmament Conference had been summoned to meet in February 1932. If that should fail, it was not to be expected that a proud and powerful nation would long submit to the thraldom in which she was held.

These humiliations, added to the cruel economic

sufferings of the people, were inevitably bringing discredit upon the democratic system that had been established in the moment of defeat. Brüning, the last of the democratic chancellors, was finding his position increasingly difficult. In the first years after the war the German people had vigorously resisted every attempt to overthrow the democratic system, and an attempt to seize power which had been made in 1922 by Adolf Hitler, the demagogic leader of a new National Socialist Party, had ended in humiliating failure. But now things were changing; patience was being exhausted; and the voting strength of the National Socialists or Nazis was increasing in an alarming way. If the self-complacent rulers of Europe desired the survival of the democratic system in Germany, which was the best hope of European peace, they must see to it that this system should be enabled to regain prestige by recovering for Germany a real equality with the other Powers; and, in particular, by ensuring the success of the Disarmament Conference. For if the armaments of the other Powers were not honestly reduced to the German level, nothing was more certain than that the armaments of Germany would presently be raised to the level of the other Powers; a new armaments race would begin, the end of which could be nothing but another and ruinous war. This was the dominating fact in the European situation, which the statesmen of other European Powers, and especially of Britain, were bound to keep in mind.

In Italy, meanwhile, the vigorous despot Mussolini was stirring up, among a hypnotised people, a fever of nationalist and militarist sentiment, a memory of the greatness of old Rome, and a readiness to redress by force the injustices from which Italy was held to be suffering. Aiming at self-sufficiency, he was striving to increase the volume of home-grown food supplies by heavy tariffs against imported foodstuffs; he was endeavouring to combat the growing volume of unemployment by immense schemes of public works, which could only be carried on by huge increases of public debt. But the outlets for Italy's manufactures were being progressively restricted by the trade barriers of other countries; she was finding more and more difficulty in paying for her needed imports of raw materials; and the standards of life of her people were being gradually lowered. She was visibly drifting towards national bankruptcy and the chaos which this would bring. The domineering spirit of Mussolini was not likely to accept such a fate; the temptation, which always besets dictators, to divert attention from domestic distresses by a "vigorous foreign policy," and to burst by force the strangling bonds by which the country was being suffocated, grew as the difficulties grew. It was soon to lead to the Abyssinian adventure, behind which, as some believed, lay grandiose schemes for the creation of an African and Mediterranean Empire, to be carved out largely at the expense of the British Power.

Other countries were suffering the same, or even greater, distresses. Even the mighty United States was passing through a period of acute economic crisis: though more nearly able to be self-sufficient than any other country, she was suffering more acutely than any of them from the dislocation of world-trade; her vast stocks of gold did nothing to relieve her distress; and she had persuaded herself that the only way to mend matters was to intensify the policy of isolation which was the ultimate cause of all these troubles.

Indeed, there was not a country in the world which did not share these sufferings, except perhaps Russia, who was beginning to emerge from the confusion of her revolution; and this led many to think that the Communist policy of Russia deserved imitation. But unrest was greatest in the countries that had suffered defeat in the war.

Austria, reduced to a tiny State with a disproportionately great city as its capital, and cut off by the tariffs of the new States from the very possibility of a healthy economic life, was for that reason in a state of acute unrest. Her natural mode of redress, as most of her citizens believed, was to be found in political and economic unity with Germany. But this was forbidden by the Versailles system, and by the power of France, which dreaded such an increment to the might of Germany: Italy also dreaded the prospect of having Germany as her nearest neighbour. Austria was therefore a perpetual source of danger in the European comity.

Hungary, deeply resenting the way in which her frontiers had been drawn after the war, and suffering from an economic distress only less grave than that of Austria, was equally a centre of unrest; and the neighbours of these disinherited States lived in a state of alarm lest trouble should arise from these quarters, and were all armed to the teeth to guard against it. In all the new States there were large subject minorities, which complained that they were oppressed by the dominant races, and that the Minority Treaties (under the guardianship of the League of Nations) were of no avail to protect them. Poland lived in dread of Russia on the one side, and on the other of Germany, whose territory was divided by the "Polish corridor."

In short, all Europe was a boiling cauldron of fears and hates and mutual suspicions, all of which were intensified and embittered by trade wars, and by the universal economic distress which they caused. An explosion anywhere might, and almost inevitably would, produce a universal conflagration, which everybody dreaded, and nobody wanted, but for which everybody was getting ready.

The responsibility for guiding Europe and the world out of this dreadful situation rested upon the League of Nations. But the League of Nations is not an independent power; it is merely the machinery through which all the nations can co-operate for common ends, if they are willing to do so. And if this co-operation was to be effective, it must be led by the greater nations which have interests in all parts of the world, by the "satisfied" nations whose vast possessions challenged the envy of the rest—although (despite their vast possessions) they were suffering equally with the rest from the consequences of unbridled economic nationalism.

There were three of the Great Powers which could have taken the lead: the United States, France, and Britain. But the United States was not even a member of the League, and was wedded to a policy of isolation. France was hag-ridden by fear of a revival of Germany, and, while loyal to the ideals of the League, conceived of it primarily as a means of preserving the *status quo* in Europe, and thus averting danger from herself. Britain alone, the greatest of the "satisfied" Powers, and the country which had most to lose from a continuance of the economic nationalism that was ruining the world, might have taken the lead; and if she had done so could have counted upon the support of almost all other States. Here was an immense opportunity, and an immense responsibility; and the Government which was faced by it was more powerfully supported at home than any other British Government in modern history. Could it rise to the greatness of this challenge, and earn the leadership and the gratitude of the world?

Four things had to be done, if the perils that threatened civilisation were to be averted. In the first place, a resort to brute force by the dissatisfied nations must be prevented, and for this purpose the authority of the League of Nations must at all costs be made operative. In the second place, the League of Nations must not be made to appear merely as a means of preserving the *status quo*, but as a means of redressing injustice. In the third place, the long-neglected promise to bring about an effective measure of all-round disarmament must be honoured. In the fourth place, the evils of economic nationalism, which was the chief and the ultimate cause of the world's troubles, must be courageously attacked, and removed or allayed.

To create a sense of security, to inspire a conviction that justice could be obtained without recourse to force, to bring about a cessation of the armaments race that threatened war and diverted the resources of the nations from the improvement of their own conditions, and, finally, to give ground for an assurance that all peoples would be enabled to share in the abundance that the fruitful earth offered—these were the highest tasks of statesmanship, and there never was a time when the performance of these tasks was more needed by the world, or more attainable by courage and imagination. The supreme test of the success of the Second National Government, to which this opportunity and this responsibility fell, is to be found in the answers to the questions how far this Government honestly tried to lead the world in the right direction, and how far it succeeded in doing so.

III

The first great test of the world's statesmanship was afforded by the aggression of Japan at the expense of China, both countries being members of the League. Japan was under an obligation, as a member of the League, not to resort to war until every possibility of peaceful settlement had been exhausted; as a signatory of the Briand-Kellogg Pact of Paris, she was pledged never to use war as an instrument of policy; as a signatory of the Nine-Power Treaty, concluded in 1922, she was pledged to respect and uphold the territorial integrity of China. Since 1922, under a Liberal Government, she had played the part of a loyal member of the League, and had apparently abandoned the vast claims on China which she had put forward during the war. Meanwhile China, under the vigorous leadership of Chiang-kai-shek, was beginning to get the better of the anarchy from which she had so long suffered.

In 1931 the policy of Japan underwent a sudden change. The Liberal Government was overthrown by the army and navy chiefs, and replaced by a Conservative Government, which in its turn was overthrown in May 1932; it was not until that date that the militarists definitely got the upper hand. What made this revolution possible was the distress from which Japan was suffering in common with the rest of the world. This made the people impatient of the existing regime, and brought popular support to the militarists; and the fact that all countries were engrossed with their own difficulties seemed to provide an opportunity for defying world opinion. On the pretext that a Japanese railway in Manchuria had suffered from Chinese sabotage, Japanese armies overran the three provinces of Manchuria, set up therein a puppet State under the name of Manchukuo, and went on to conquer the wide province of Jehol; and when this violence was met in China by a general boycott of Japanese goods, a Japanese army proceeded to use the foreign settlements of Shanghai as a base for an attack upon the heart of China.

Here was a challenge to the system of peace which could not be disregarded without bringing that system down in ruins. If the League should fail to come to the aid of China (which appealed for its assistance) no country would be likely to trust to the League for its defence, and the Disarmament Conference would be condemned to failure. If this wholesale repudiation of pledges were to be accepted, no trust could henceforth be placed in the pledges of nations, and without such trust no structure of peace could last.

Apart from the distress from which the whole world was suffering, the circumstances were extremely favourable for resistance to this challenge. The two Great Powers which were still outside of the League, the United States and Russia, were both deeply concerned to check Japanese aggression, and were likely to be willing to take common action for this purpose.

Equally with these two, Britain was deeply interested in the preservation of Chinese independence. It naturally fell to Britain to take the lead. It is probable that a prompt and united demonstration of world opinion hostile to this kind of action would have sufficed to give pause to the Japanese militarists, not yet firmly in the saddle. But if further action was necessary, a general embargo upon Japanese imports and a prohibition of the export of petrol to Japan would pretty certainly have brought Japan to book, without any necessity for military action.

An opportunity for securing combined action, and especially for securing the invaluable co-operation of the United States, came in January 1932, when the American Secretary of State sent a note to Japan refusing recognition for any acquisitions of territory made by force and in defiance of obligations, and invited the co-operation of Britain. It is more than probable that if Britain had agreed, all other countries, including Russia, would have joined in the demonstration; and if Japan had still remained defiant, common action of a more drastic kind, such as the withdrawal of ambassadors and the imposition of an embargo on Japanese goods, would have become possible. But the British Government, without even waiting to take counsel with other Powers, very promptly replied that they did not propose to take any such action, because Japan had promised to maintain the open door for trade in Manchuria! This was to sell the collective system for a mess of pottage; and in the event we got the mess, but not the pottage. For the puppet State of Manchukuo announced that only countries which recognised it as a legitimate Government could expect to enjoy trading facilities.

Far from taking the lead in pressing for effective action against Japan, the British Government appeared to regard the Japanese proceedings with benevolent neutrality. The Foreign Secretary, Sir John Simon, publicly declared his sympathy with Japan. He is said to have stated that the Japanese action was "technically wrong, but morally justified;" and he was thanked by the head of the Japanese delegation at Geneva for having stated the Japanese case better than he himself could have stated it. The only positive action taken by the Government was to prohibit the export of munitions *to both combatants*. This was, in effect, an aid to Japan, who had munition factories of her own, while China depended upon importation. But the embargo was maintained only for a short time: profits were being lost. The chief motive of the British Government was a dread of being drawn into a war in the Far East: they feared that if Japan were annoyed, she might attack Hong Kong or Singapore. It was in the last degree improbable that Japan would commit this folly, especially if all the Powers had been acting together. Nevertheless the Government took credit for having avoided the danger of war, and charged those who advocated effective League action with a bellicose readiness to plunge into war.

In face of this attitude, adopted by the Power that was most deeply concerned in Eastern affairs, the League did nothing to help China, or to check the aggression of Japan. A Commission of Inquiry, containing representatives of five nations, was sent out to study the problem, and spent several months in doing so. Its admirable and unanimous report condemned the action of Japan, but also made proposals which would have met all her reasonable claims, and would at the same time have secured to China a chance of reorganisation and consolidation under the guidance of the League. China accepted this scheme; Japan contemptuously rejected it; the League members unanimously endorsed it, but took no further action; whereupon Japan withdrew from the League. Since then, with complete contempt for the League and its ideals, Japan has continued her pressure upon China, and this pressure has defeated the struggles of China to consolidate her system. Japan has now announced a sort of Monroe Doctrine for the Far East, claiming for herself a dominant position in that vast and populous quarter of the world. It is not unlikely that those who were opposed to bringing pressure upon Japan lest she should attack Hong Kong may in the future find themselves forced to defend that island, and other Western footholds in the East, against a much more formidable Power than that before which they cowered in trembling impotence in 1932; and may find that, when that time comes, a ruined collective system will be of no avail to help them.

The successful Japanese aggression was an almost fatal blow to the prestige and influence of the League of Nations. It involved the betrayal of China, which had trusted to the League. It involved the submissive acceptance of shameless breaches of treaties, and therefore the undermining of the very foundations of international agreement. It taught the other nations of the world two things: first, that they would be foolish to look to the League for protection, and therefore that any large measure of disarmament would be dangerous; and, secondly, that a Power which was prepared to dishonour its pledges could safely do so, counting upon the short-sighted selfishness and timidity of the Powers which most loudly professed loyalty to the ideal of collective security. That these lessons had been throughly learnt was to be demonstrated by the events of the next four years. As a Chinese delegate said at Geneva, during the last four years "the sky has been black with chickens coming home to roost."

The Second National Government cannot be held solely responsible for this disaster. But it has the largest share of responsibility, because it had a better chance of taking the lead than any other Government, and deliberately rejected it. It was so much afraid, that it refused even to try to bring about united action among the nations, either for the purpose of making moral pressure effective, or for the purpose of bringing economic sanctions into operation. The results of this failure were all but irreparable; and that fateful week in January 1932, when Sir John Simon turned down the approach made by America towards collective action, may come to be regarded as one of the most disastrous turning-points in history.

IV

We have noted that the failure to deal firmly with Japan almost ensured the failure of the Disarmament Conference. But when the Conference met in February 1932, this failure was not yet apparent: the Lytton Commission had still to make its report, and it had still to be seen whether the League would act upon this report. At this moment, if the nations of Europe, and the United States of America, who made it plain that she would co-operate on this issue, had succeeded in reaching an agreement on disarmament, the collective system would have been immensely strengthened, and common action to uphold it would have been practicable.

The whole world desired the success of the Conference. All the nations awaited a clear lead, such as America had given in the only successful disarmament conference held since the war, the Naval Conference of Washington in 1922. It was from Britain that a lead was expected; a British statesman, Mr. Arthur Henderson, occupied the chair; and the opening speech was assigned to the British Foreign Secretary, Sir John Simon. Instead of imitating the boldness of the American Secretary of State in 1922, he contented himself with a string of vague platitudes. A member of the British delegation has recorded the impression which this speech produced. "I shall never forget the icy dismay which greeted a speech containing no word or hint of constructive or considered policy. . . . We had been offered the leadership, and allowed it to slip through our fingers."

The best way of approach to the problem of disarmament would have been that all the other nations should agree to accept the provision which had been applied to Germany, whereby she was forbidden to possess the so-called "aggressive" weapons—big battleships, submarines, big guns, fighting aeroplanes, and tanks. Italy actually proposed this. Britain proposed a resolution approving in principle of "qualitative disarmament," but then left the matter to be discussed by the naval and military "experts." They had found no difficulty in 1919 in laying down definitions in the case of Germany; but they found insuperable difficulties in 1932 in applying the same definitions to their own countries. The only "aggressive" weapon which the British Government was prepared to abolish was the submarine, which is very inconvenient for Britain; but other countries, regarding the submarine as the best means of keeping big battleships at arm's length, would not agree unless battleships were also abolished, and to this Britain would not agree—one of the British experts declaring that battleships were "more precious than rubies" to those who possessed them.

"Qualitative" disarmament having broken down, largely owing to the attitude of Britain, the American President, Mr. Hoover, tried to give a fresh start to the Conference with a proposal that all countries should reduce their existing battleships by one-third, and their cruisers and destroyers by one-quarter; while no country was to have more than 35,000 tons of submarines; and big guns, tanks, and bombing aircraft were to be abolished. Part of these proposals were turned down by Britain on the ground that Japan would not agree, and might leave the Conference if this was insisted upon; thus Japan, the defier of the Covenant, was made the arbiter of the Conference, whereas the object of loyal statesmanship should have been to isolate her. As for battleships, Britain proposed that they should all be retained until the expiration of the naval treaties, and should then be replaced by rather smaller but improved ships.

Again, France proposed that there should be a limitation of the amount to be spent on armaments, that the manufacture of arms should be brought under international control, that all air-forces should be abolished, that civil aviation should be brought under international control, and that an international air police force should be created to prevent abuses. The British Government opposed all these proposals.

These details may appear tedious. But they are necessary to show that in all the early stages of the Conference the British Government offered no sort of leadership, but confined itself to criticising, opposing, or minimising the proposals put forward by other Powers.

In March 1933, when the complete success of Japan's defiance of the League was fully apparent, and the utter failure of the Disarmament Conference seemed all but inevitable, the British Government seems at last to have awakened to a sense of the gravity of the situation. For the first time it took the initiative, by proposing a Draft Convention, in which an attempt was made to set forth a series of compromises with the various proposals that had been put forward; but it said nothing about budgetary limitation, or international supervision and control, or the private manufacture of arms. The Draft Convention was accepted as a basis for discussion; but by this time the Conference had lost heart, and nothing came of it. In May, however, America once more attempted to galvanise the Conference into life. President Roosevelt, while accepting the British Draft Convention as a first step, proposed a plan for fixing time limits for the abolition of the most dangerous aggressive weapons, notably fighting aeroplanes. Even Hitler, now in power in Germany, accepted the Roosevelt plan as the basis for a Disarmament Convention. Yet more important than these proposals was an offer from America to consult with other Powers when there was danger of war, and to make plans for concerted action. This might have been the means of giving renewed strength to the collective system. But the British Government received these proposals with a chill disdain: it made no response either to the proposals for progressive limitation, or to those for collective action. Indeed, throughout the Conference, all the American proposals were treated by the British Government with a scarcely veiled contempt.

The Disarmament Conference was by this time doomed to failure: every hope of a general agreement for all-round reduction had been destroyed. But there were two special subjects on which it was still hoped that agreement might be reached. One was the abolition of warfare in the air—the ugliest nightmare of modern war. All nations realised the horrible nature of this peril. Yet in the Air Committee of the Conference the British representatives confined themselves to raising every kind of objection, and made not a single constructive proposal. Nevertheless, on May 27, 1933, the Conference almost came to an agreement on the abolition of national air-forces and the international control of civil aviation, which had been persistently advocated by France. Agreement would almost certainly have been reached if Britain had been willing to withdraw her insistence that bombing aeroplanes should be legal in outlying territories, and her objection to the international control of aviation. In maintaining this position, and thus wrecking the chance of saving the world from the worst horrors of war, Britain had the support of only two States—Iraq and Siam. This was, in effect, the death-blow of the Conference. Speaking later (May 1935) in the House of Lords, the Air Minister, Lord Londonderry, took credit for having played an important part in defeating the plan for the abolition of bombing aeroplanes. "I had the utmost difficulty," he said, "amid the public outcry, in preserving the use of the bombing aeroplane, *even* on the frontiers of the Middle East and India.... I am not recalling these things in any spirit of personal pride and self-glorification. I am stating facts."

The other question upon which agreement might have been reached was the control of the traffic in arms. Here America took the lead, for her citizens had been horrified by the revelations made in the Senate inquiry regarding the methods by which this blood-traffic is pursued. But France, Russia, and other countries were equally keen. Even when the Disarmament Commission was manifestly expiring, America strove to get some agreement on this head, urging the adoption of a separate Convention to regulate the traffic in arms, under the supervision of a Permanent Disarmament Commission. Once again America was offering co-operation with the League. But the proposal was defeated by the opposition of Britain, supported by Japan and Italy.

No attempt has here been made to follow in detail the pitiful history of the Disarmament Conference. But enough has been said to show that the British Government never attempted—save in the abortive Draft Convention in March 1933—to give the lead which the rest of the world expected her to give, but on the contrary limited herself to negative and destructive criticism. It is the "considered opinion" of a member of the British Delegation who attended the Conference throughout, that "the British Government carries the main responsibility for having wrecked the Disarmament Conference." This is a formidable judgment, all the more formidable when it is remembered that the fate of civilisation may well have been determined by the failure of this Conference.

It is, indeed, constantly and loudly claimed that

Britain did at least lead the way in disarming herself; that she went so far in "unilateral disarmament" as to endanger her own security; and that no other country followed her lead. But other countries do not admit this. A rough test may be found by comparing the gross expenditure of the Great Powers on armaments, in comparison with their expenditure on the eve of the Great War. In 1934 Japan's expenditure was three times as great as it was in 1914; the expenditure of Italy was rather more than 50 per cent higher than in 1914; the expenditure of France and Britain was almost exactly 50 per cent higher; the expenditure of the United States rather less than 50 per cent higher. In face of these figures, it is not easy to maintain the contention that Britain alone has virtuously reduced her armaments.

V

Just as the failure to deal firmly with Japan almost ensured the failure of the Disarmament Conference, so the failure of the Disarmament Conference brought the German problem to an acute stage, and helped to bring about the downfall of democracy in Germany and the establishment of the Nazi Dictatorship.

At the outset of the Conference, Brüning, the Chancellor of democratic Germany, had declared that two things were essential: firstly, Germany must have "equality of status" and be treated on the same basis as other Powers; and, secondly, this equality must be brought about by the reduction of the armaments of other Powers, rather than by an increase of the armaments of Germany. If this had been accepted, even in principle, the prestige of the democratic system might have been strengthened in Germany and its downfall averted. The German Government, indeed, indicated that it could not go on with the Conference unless the principle of "equality of status" were granted. Yet at the end of the first session of the Conference Sir John Simon gave elaborate reasons for postponing any decision—postponement being the British Government's panacea for all difficulties. The result was that Germany withdrew from the Disarmament Conference.

Germany was persuaded to return when, in December 1932, the British, French, Italian, and American Governments agreed that any disarmament convention must be based on "equality of rights in a system which would provide security for all nations." Germany would not come in without equality of rights. But France would not come in without some guarantee of security; and the British Government, while willing to accept any formula, was not willing to accept any commitments such as were necessary if there was to be any real guarantee of security.

In March 1933 the Nazi Revolution took place in Germany, and the British and French Governments found that they had to deal with a very different spirit from that which had marked the previous democratic Government. As soon as he came to power, Hitler began to rearm—defying the Treaty of Versailles, but able to argue that since "equality of rights" had been promised, and no attempt had been made by the other Powers to bring it about by their own disarmament, Germany was entitled to rearm. It was in these circumstances that the British Draft Convention was brought forward, and supplemented by the more courageous proposals of President Roosevelt. Hitler announced his readiness to accept these proposals as a basis; and a little later he stated that he would forgo every weapon which the other Powers would give up, and submit to any restrictions which they would accept.

Meanwhile, the Draft Convention had come to nothing because the British Government would not accept any security commitments; the Conference had been suspended, and the discussion was proceeding privately among the Great Powers. On October 14, 1933, Sir John Simon put forward a proposal that no reductions should be made for four years, in order that time might be given to see how Germany behaved herself. In face of this, it is not surprising that Germany withdrew from the Conference and from the League, and rapidly intensified the work of rearmament.

This frightened the British Government, which showed once again that it would always yield to a bully what it would not yield to reason. In January 1934, without having made any previous agreement with France, it offered to agree to a large increase of the German land-army (which threatened France), asked for a postponement of any decision about air-armaments (which might threaten Britain), and said nothing about sea armaments (which would certainly threaten Britain). This naturally angered France, who felt that she was being betrayed by Britain. When Hitler showed some readiness to accept the British proposal (with modifications), France emphatically refused to agree, and set to work to organise security in Europe by means of agreements with some of the Eastern Powers, by making friends with Italy and by bringing Russia into the League—the first step towards the new Franco-Russian alliance which was concluded in 1936. Again, in 1935 the British Government concluded a Naval Agreement with Germany, without consulting other Powers, whereby Germany was to have a fleet 35 per cent of that of Britain. This still further angered France.

Meanwhile, as we have seen in an earlier chapter, the World Economic Conference had also broken down in 1933; and with its breakdown had disappeared the hope of lightening the economic strains which were ultimately the main cause of the political stresses of the period, and which were driving the dispossessed Powers to desperation. As we have seen, the British Government had been expected to take the lead in this sphere, as in the Disarmament Conference, and had failed to do so. Its attitude would have ensured the failure of the Economic Conference even if there had been no other difficulties.

VI

In the summer and autumn of 1934, therefore, the outlook on all sides was deeply perturbing to all who had hoped that the system of the League of Nations would give peace to the world. The League had not been used to prevent dissatisfied Powers from resorting to force; it had not been used to redress injustices— so far as these had been ameliorated, the amelioration was due to defiance of the League rather than to its action; the attempt to secure disarmament had miserably failed, after ten years of waiting and preparation; and nothing had been done to remove the economic difficulties which were the main source of the trouble. In the East Japan had defied the League with complete success; treaty obligations (the sanctity of which is the foundation of international order) had been repudiated with impunity and almost without protest; in Europe

Germany was rearming in hot haste, and all the other Powers were making ready to follow her example; and new alliances, like those which preceded and caused the Great War, were being formed.

The League seemed to have failed. Yet it was not the League which had failed; it was the Great Powers, without whose leadership the League system could not be made effective, which had failed to use the machinery of the League with the requisite courage and imagination. Among them all, the heaviest, though not the sole, responsibility lay upon Britain, to whom the world had looked in vain for leadership. Under her National Government Britain had shown a timidity, a vacillation, a lack of faith, which by no means represented the spirit of the people.

Feeling this and lamenting it, the friends of the League system in Britain resolved to undertake a great attempt to demonstrate the real sentiment of the British people on this subject, by taking a ballot vote of the whole electorate. It was a bold experiment to attempt such a thing without the excitement and the intense publicity of a General Election; indeed, it was a new experiment in democracy to try to elicit the opinion of the electorate on a single isolated subject without calling upon the machinery of a party fight. The enterprise received every discouragement from the Government; the Foreign Secretary publicly denounced it; the Conservative Party refused to co-operate in carrying it out, though some Conservative members gave it their support; the great bulk of the newspaper press poured ridicule upon it, and advised the electors to tear up the ballot-papers. Nevertheless, by the labours of some fifty thousand voluntary workers, the ballot was carried through, at a cost which formed but a minute fraction of the cost of a General Election. And although the voting was not, and could not be, complete, nearly 11½ million voters filled up ballot-papers, and gave a stupendous majority in favour of a League policy—in favour of disarmament by agreement among the nations, in favour of the abolition of air-warfare, in favour of the abolition of private profit in the manufacture and sale of armaments, in favour of common action against an aggressor, by economic sanctions in the first instance, and if necessary, in the last resort, by military measures.

The Peace Ballot made it abundantly clear that the preponderant opinion of the British people strongly supported a policy of collective action for the enforcement of peace, such as the National Government had failed adequately to support, even if it had not caused its failure. The result of the Peace Ballot was remarkable. Within a month of its conclusion, the National Government had been reconstructed (June 1935), Sir John Simon had ceased to be Foreign Secretary, and a new Cabinet Office, that of Minister for League of Nations Affairs, had been created, and assigned to Mr. Anthony Eden, who (as Under-Secretary for Foreign Affairs) had distinguished himself by his loyalty to the ideals of the League, and had done as much as a subordinate minister could do to keep British policy on sound League lines.

This change was no sooner made than Britain and the other Powers were faced by a new problem, that of Italian ambitions at the expense of Abyssinia, which had indeed been threatening for some time, but now reached an acute stage.

VII

The ancient Christian Empire of Abyssinia—a rugged land of high mountains in Eastern Africa, surrounded by belts of desert land—is the only part of Africa that has hitherto resisted European conquest. In the last decade of the nineteenth century Italy, having acquired, as her sole share of the African partition, two coastal strips, Eritrea and Italian Somaliland, on the north and south of Abyssinia, had tried to conquer the country, but had met with humiliating defeat. The coloured peoples of Africa, and indeed of the world, regarded Abyssinia with pride as the only country which had been able to resist the white man's domination. It was a backward land, in which domestic slavery still survived. But an enlightened Emperor, Haile Selassie, had set himself to civilise his country, and was eager to obtain the help of the European peoples in this task, so long as this did not entail the loss of independence. In 1926 he had succeeded in obtaining admission as a member of the League of Nations, and hoped through the League to obtain the help which he needed, without forfeiting his country's freedom. At that date Britain was doubtful about the admission of Abyssinia to the League, having suffered a good deal from the slave-raids of uncontrolled Abyssinian chieftains in Kenya and the Soudan. The chief supporters of Abyssinia's application in 1926 were Italy and France. This seemed to show that Italy had abandoned her dreams of conquest: the more so since she had also concluded with Abyssinia a treaty whereunder all disputes between them were to be submitted to arbitration. Under the guardianship of the League, it might seem, Abyssinia could hope to make progress in civilisation, and to introduce Western methods of organisation without sacrificing her freedom.

In 1934 the Italian dictator, Mussolini, reversed his policy, and despite the sworn obligations which he had undertaken through the admission of Abyssinia to the League, through his special treaty with that country, and through his undertaking under the Pact of Paris never to use war as an instrument of policy, decided to undertake the conquest of Abyssinia. The motives for this change are easily perceived. Italy was in a grave economic position, and unless something was done the popularity of the Fascist regime might dwindle. Markets for Italian products were being restricted by the tariffs of other countries, notably Britain, and the World Economic Conference had done nothing to redress the situation. Access to needed tropical raw materials had been restricted by the Ottawa Agreements. Perhaps Abyssinia would fill the gaps; at any rate, the Italian people might think so. The successful defiance of the League by Japan and by Germany, and the pitiful failure of the Disarmament Conference, seemed to show that the League could safely be defied. So the conquest of Abyssinia was projected; and a frontier incident at Wal-Wal, in which the Italians were almost certainly in the wrong, and which in any case ought to have been settled under the terms of the arbitration treaty, provided the excuse.

From September 1934 onwards, Italian troops and supplies were gradually accumulated in Eritrea and Italian Somaliland. Abyssinia saw what was coming, and appealed to the League for the protection to which she was entitled. The League made no response. If it had from the outset been made clear to Mussolini that Britain would take her League obligations seriously, and would do her best to secure common action against the aggressor, it is pretty certain that the Duce would have hesitated, and perhaps abandoned his dishonourable plans: he later complained that no warning had been given to him. But nothing was done, save that the exportation of munitions to both contestants from Britain was prohibited—an action which, as in the case of China and Japan, favoured the aggressor; for Abyssinia was without modern armaments, and Italy was amply equipped. In June 1935, when the Italian intentions were abundantly clear, and Italian troops were passing through the Red Sea, France, Britain, and Italy held a conference at Stresa, to plan concerted action against Germany. We have been informed that the British representatives at that conference were accompanied by experts on the Abyssinian question. But the question was not raised —because Mussolini did not raise it, and the directors of British policy were apparently afraid of offending him. It is probable that if Britain had spoken firmly, even at this late date, the horrors of the Abyssinian war might have been averted.

Almost at this moment, however, came the remarkable result of the Peace Ballot in Britain, followed by the reconstruction of the National Government. The result was that in September, when the Italian attack on Abyssinia was about to begin, the new British Foreign Secretary, Sir Samuel Hoare, made a speech at Geneva which electrified the world. He announced that Britain intended to keep her pledged word, and to take the lead in bringing the strength of the League to bear against the aggressor. This announcement brought about a demonstration of the eagerness with which the world had been awaiting a lead from Britain. Fifty nations declared their readiness to take part in common action against the aggressor. Everywhere—not only in Europe but in the United States, in the British Dominions, and in the colonies inhabited by coloured peoples, who deeply sympathised with Abyssinia—there was enthusiasm for the new policy. At last, it seemed, the League of Nations was to be justified, and proved to be worthy of the trust of the nations. At last the efficacy of "economic sanctions" was to be tested. With surprising unanimity fifty nations agreed to impose restrictions upon their trade with Italy, in many cases to their own serious detriment.

The enthusiasm was so great that the National Government decided to take advantage of it by precipitating a General Election and securing a new tenure of power. They did so, very hastily, in October, and obtained an overwhelming majority. At the same time they demanded and obtained from the electorate power to carry out an indefinite programme of rearmament, in order to be in a position to defend the "collective system," should Italy be so mad as to attack the banded Powers of the world.

The sanctions at first imposed, however, though they were likely to cause grave inconvenience to Italy and to increase her economic distress, were not of a kind likely to interfere seriously with the conduct of the war. Additional sanctions of this kind were under consideration before the British General Election: in particular, the importation of petrol into Italy was to be prohibited, and this prohibition, if effective, would have crippled the Italian air fleet and tanks, in which she had a complete superiority over the Abyssinians.

Unfortunately, France was reluctant to join in these measures; she had put difficulties in the way of even the first sanctions. The reason was that, after what had happened in the last few years, she had lost faith in the League, and especially in Britain. For that reason, as a security against the growing military power of Germany, she had made friends with Italy, and had made an agreement with her in January 1935, the precise character of which has never been revealed, but there is a widespread belief that she had promised Italy a free hand in Abyssinia. She was loth to weaken these new ties, which she would probably never have made if she had not been convinced that Britain could not be trusted, and if she had not been perturbed by the British attitude during the disarmament conference and the discussions about German rearmament. Her Foreign Secretary, M. Laval, therefore interposed all sorts of obstacles in the way of the imposition of the oil and metal sanctions, which alone could be effective in stopping the war. Nevertheless, if she had been forced to make a choice, there is little doubt that France would have clung to the League, now that its strength was reviving. In any case, France is not an oil-producing country. Her reluctance would have been more than outbalanced if America, the greatest oil-producing country, had been ready to join in the embargo. And, in spite of all the rebuffs which America had received, President Roosevelt made it plain that he would interpret the neutrality which was imposed upon him by the American Senate in such a way as to prohibit the export to Italy of more oil than was normally exported to her in peace-time. And as Italy normally drew only a small proportion of her peace-time supplies from the United States, this, combined with an embargo imposed by the other oil-producing countries, would have ensured the crippling of the Italian campaign, and the first great victory of the League of Nations over an aggressive Power.

The prestige, perhaps even the survival, of the League of Nations, and the prestige of Britain, who had for the first time taken a definite initiative in favour of a League policy, depended upon resolute action at this juncture. But the Government was apparently incapable of firm action. Less than a month after the General Election, which had been won on the assurance that the Government would resolutely pursue a League policy, the new Foreign Secretary, Sir Samuel Hoare, paid a week-end visit to Paris, and came to an agreement with the French Government whereby Italy was to be offered generous peace terms at the expense of Abyssinia—terms far more generous than those which had been rejected at the beginning of the war. The aggressor was to be rewarded, at the cost of his victim, for his defiance of treaty obligations and of the League. No doubt the reason for this was an anticipation of the German aggression which was soon to follow: Italy, aggressor or not, was needed (according to these timorous statesmen) to make weight against Germany.

The Hoare-Laval agreement produced, as it well might, an outcry of contemptuous anger in all classes and parties in Britain. There has seldom been a more unanimous expression of public opinion, and even the omnipotent National Government had to give way before it. Sir Samuel Hoare, the hero of September, had to resign; the Prime Minister, though equally responsible, clung to his post, but with a terrible loss of prestige. Mr. Anthony Eden, who alone seemed to have done his best to uphold the cause of the League, became Foreign Secretary. But the blow to British prestige throughout the world was very serious. It was now more difficult than ever to press on with effective sanctions; it began to appear doubtful whether the existing sanctions could be maintained. The revived vigour of the League was destroyed. And, seizing his opportunity, Hitler proceeded to send German armies into the demilitarised Rhineland, realising that the best way of dealing with the nerveless statesmen who directed European affairs was to present them with *faits accomplis*. It had been demonstrated beyond challenge that, with these people, the bully could always get his way.

Meanwhile, with shame and humiliation, we have had to watch the progress of the cruel war in Abyssinia. The Italians, knowing that they had nothing to fear, went on from iniquity to iniquity. Their airmen deliberately bombed British and Swedish Red Cross hospitals in order to prevent them from helping the unhappy Abyssinians. This led to mild protests; one cannot but ask oneself how such an outrage would have been dealt with by earlier British Governments. Air-squadrons deliberately bombarded open and independent towns and villages, slaughtering unarmed peasants, women, and children. Worst of all, Italy shamelessly repudiated the solemn agreement to which she and other nations had pledged their word, never under any circumstances to use poison gas as a weapon of war; and gas-bombs were launched from the skies upon the doomed Abyssinians, causing thousands of men, women, and children to die in unspeakable torture. Against these modes of attack a primitive people had no means of resistance: their gallant defence, which had long delayed the Italian onslaught, broke down; and it seemed that the ruthless aggressor would win a complete victory. The League humbly besought him to negotiate for peace. His insolent reply was that he must first subjugate the whole of Abyssinia, and that he would negotiate only with the conquered people, permitting no interference by the League.

In truth, deserted and unaided by the civilized Powers to which they had trusted, the Abyssinians could offer no further organized resistance. Their capital was occupied by the Italians, who now controlled the eastern half of the country. Their Emperor fled, first to Palestine, then to Britain, where he was received with warmth by the crowds, but with chill disregard by the Government.

What was now to be done? The rulers of the Great Powers had expected Abyssinia to fight the battle of the League for them unaided, and to hold out long enough to force Italy to accept a League solution. They were disappointed. Were they now to continue the struggle on their own account? It was evident that Italy had been reduced to grave distress even by the inadequate "sanctions" hitherto imposed. If these sanctions were continued, still more if they were intensified, it might still be possible to teach her, and through her the world, that aggression did not pay: it might still be possible to show that the "collective system" could not be defied with impunity. On the other hand, the proud rulers of Britain were obsessed by the fear of war. They dreaded the outbreak of fresh trouble on the side of Germany. They wanted to be able to count upon aid from Italy should this come about. It did not occur to them that nothing could give a more powerful stimulus to the warlike elements in Germany than proof of their weakness in dealing with another and less formidable Power. It did not occur to them that it was dangerous to trust a Government which had shown that it did not hold itself bound by any treaties or by the most solemn obligations of honour. Terrified by the strong will of Mussolini, they decided that it was necessary—whatever the consequences—to accept defeat. Having, seven months earlier, led fifty nations into a conflict for the maintenance of law and justice, the British Government decided to advise a precipitate retreat, to recommend the withdrawal of the sanctions already imposed, and to persuade the League of Nations to submit to the aggressor and acknowledge its own impotence. This meant that the best hope of security against a war which, if it comes, must bring ruin to civilization, was undermined, if not finally destroyed; and Britain voluntarily accepted the worst humiliation which she has ever had to undergo. Such were the results, to their own country and to the world, of the foreign policy pursued by the National Government.

VIII

The gravest condemnation of the National Government is to be found in the terrible worsening of the position in Europe and the world which has come about during its period of office. It would be unfair to attribute to it the *sole* responsibility for this state of things. But it had the opportunity of leading the world in the right direction, and—except for a brief moment in the autumn of 1935, which was soon followed by a relapse into the old timorous inaction—it has refused to give the lead for which the world was waiting. The prestige of the League of Nations has been so reduced by successive failures that it has lost the confidence of the world. The attempt to bring about disarmament has utterly broken down, and all the nations, led by Germany, are arming to the teeth. The willingness of America to co-operate has been repeatedly rebuffed. The ruinous policy of economic nationalism—more ruinous to Britain than to any other country—is rampant still, and nothing has been done to reduce the fever. No attempt of any kind has been made to deal with the restrictions that are strangling the dissatisfied countries, and they have been taught to look to force rather than to negotiation for relief from their distresses. All these disasters, which may culminate in the ruin of our civilisation, could have been averted: every people, almost every Government, was aware of them, and eager to avert them. What was needed was resolute and courageous leadership; and the one Power in the world in a position to give this leadership was Britain. Under the National Government, she failed at every point to give it.

It has, indeed, been very difficult to determine what the policy of Britain under the National Government actually was, and this uncertainty has unquestionably contributed to produce the confusion of international politics. Time and again spokesmen of the Government have asserted that support of the League of Nations was the foundation of their policy. But they have not recognised that the other nations expect leadership from the Great Powers: always, except in September 1935, they have shrunk from the responsibility of leadership; and even on that occasion they trembled away from the position they had at first taken up.

More important, they have never made it clear how far they were prepared to go in support of the League system, and what contribution they were prepared to make to the establishment of collective security. Britain's uncertainty on this point has produced uncertainty in other nations, and the League has become a trembling jelly, which every bully felt he could safely defy. In the last analysis, the fundamental question which has never been fairly put even to the British people, and never fairly answered, is the question, What is Britain prepared to fight for, in the last resort, if fighting becomes necessary? There are extreme pacifists who would have us declare that we will never fight in any circumstances. That is a logically tenable position, which would be logically followed by complete unilateral disarmament. But the Government does not take this view. It maintains great armaments, which it would not do unless it believed that fighting might become necessary. Presumably Britain would fight to resist invasion. But apparently she will not fight, not even with fifty nations on her side, to preserve, a system that would make invasion impossible? Presumably she would fight to defend any part of the British Empire, such as Kenya, or the Falkland Islands. But would she fight to defend the collective system of peace, the creation and preservation of which is far more important for her than the possession of the Falkland Islands? Apparently not: not even if the greater part of the world were arrayed upon her side.

Kenya and the Falkland Islands are almost safe from attack because all the world knows that the whole might of the British Empire would be brought into the field for their defence. They would be still safer, and China and Abyssinia and other countries would be safe also, if all the world knew that any attack upon them would, if necessary, bring into the field not only the might of the British Empire, but the might of other countries as well. It is only because this is *not* made clear to the world that wars of aggression take place at all. To make it clear that Britain and other loyal members of the League will if need be fight for the maintenance of the collective system is *not* to run the risk of being drawn into frequent wars; it is to reduce the risk of war to a minimum. It is by wavering on this vital point, so that nobody has known what she will do, that Britain has been largely responsible for bringing the collective system into disrepute, and increasing immensely the danger of war.

INDEX

Abyssinian adventure, the, 168, 188, 189, 191 *et seq.*
Africa, South: self-government in, 68
Agricultural labourers, 133, 141, 142
Agricultural Marketing Act, 65, 67, 140
Agricultural policy, 131 *et seq.*
America. *See* United States
Anomalies Act, 21, 88
Austin, Sir H., 123

Balance of Trade, 99–109
Baldwin, Mr., 14, 15, 17, 18, 19, 20, 21, 23, 25, 26, 28, 29, 30, 33, 37, 38, 43, 44, 45, 48, 50, 51, 54, 74, 143, 154
Balfour Committee on Trade, 124, 125, 127
Bank of England, 23, 24, 25, 32, 81, 82
Beaverbrook, Lord, 143
Belgium, 62, 63
Bessemer (steel) process, 121
"Better Way to Better Times," A, 94, 95
Black-coated unemployment, 56
Board of Trade, 103, 104, 107, 122, 128
Boot trade, 118–19
Brewers' profits, 20
Briand-Kellogg Pact, the, 172
Brüning, 183

Budget, the, 18, 20, 24, 25, 26, 28, 29, 30, 34, 35, 43, 52, 73, 74, 77, 80
Building, activity in house, 58

Chamberlain, Mr., 63, 73, 74, 75, 76, 77, 109, 110, 113, 115, 117, 118, 122, 124
Chiang-Kai-Shek, 172
China, 10, 172, 173, 175, 176, 177
Churchill, Winston, 15, 20, 21, 33
Coal Industry, 120
Conservative dictatorship, 49, 67
Conservatives, 18, 21, 27, 32, 36, 37, 40, 41, 42, 44–5, 46, 47, 49, 50, 53, 54, 57, 68, 134, 187
Cosgrave, Mr., 68
Coupons, 28, 45, 46, 47, 48
Courtaulds, 120
Crisis of 1929, the, 9, 10, 13, 14, 17, 20, 21, 22

Dawes settlement, 166
Debts, International, 12, 14, 22
Derating Act of 1929, 18
de Valera, Mr., 68, 69
Disarmament Conference, 166, 167, 173, 177, 178, 179, 180, 181, 182, 183, 184, 186, 190
Distressed Areas, 95, 116–17

Economic Conference, International, 59–60, 62, 64, 84, 87, 94, 186, 190
"Economic nationalism," 10
Economy Act, 30
Eden, Anthony, 188, 194
Election, the General, of 1931, 40 *et seq.*, 55
Elliot, W., 64, 140, 141
Empire Free Trade, 143
Entertainment tax, 75
Exchange Equalisation Fund, 81

Fascist idea, 66
Finance, National, 23, 50, 73 *et seq.*
Fiscal policy, change of, 43, 52
Foreign policy, 161
France, 12, 13, 15, 25, 32, 61
Franco-Russian Alliance, 185
Free Trade, 45, 46, 47, 48, 50, 51, 53, 105, 107, 111, 112, 118, 119, 124, 129, 130

George, Mr. Lloyd, 37, 47, 49, 82, 94, 96, 97
Germany, 11, 12, 14, 22, 23, 33, 40, 74, 163, 165, 166, 167, 183, 184
Gold Standard, 10, 11, 13, 15, 25, 26, 31, 32, 33, 34, 36, 41, 43, 55, 57, 61, 63, 81, 98, 106, 112
Government employees, reduction in pay of, 30, 31, 75
Government of India Act, 67, 68
Great War, the, 9, 10, 11, 12, 14, 187
Gullett, Mr., 147

Haile Selassie, 189
Henderson, Arthur, 178
Hitler, 167, 180, 184, 185, 195
Hoare, Sir Samuel, 159, 191, 194
Holland, 62, 63
Hoover, Mr., 179
Hull, Mr. Cordell, 60
Hume, D., 37
Hunter, Sir J., 123

Incitement to Sedition Bill, 66, 67
Income-Tax, 31, 75, 76
India, 67, 68
Invergordon, threat of mutiny at, 32
Ireland, 68, 69
Iron and steel industry, 120, 121, 123
Italy, 12, 24, 71, 163; and Abyssinia, 189 *et seq.*

Japan, 9, 163, 164, 165, 172, 173, 174, 175, 176, 177, 179, 180, 183, 186, 190

Labour Government, 18, 21, 22, 24, 25, 26, 27, 36, 37, 41–2, 46, 47, 49, 87
Lausanne, 22, 166
Laval, M., 193, 194
Law, Bonar, 14
League of Nations, 57, 59, 69, 155, 170, 171, 186, 187, 188, 189, 192, 198, 199
Lee, Sir Kenneth, 126
Liberals, 37, 39, 45, 46, 47, 50, 52, 53, 54, 94

London Chamber of Commerce, 122
Londonderry, Lord, 181
Luxemburg, 62, 63
Lytton Commission, 177

MacDonald, Ramsay, 21, 28, 29, 30, 41, 42, 45, 47, 48, 50
McKenna duties, 78, 111
May Committee, the, 23
Means Test, 89, 92
Milk Scheme, 137–8
Monetary system, disorganisation of, 10, 11
Monte Video, 62
Morris, Sir W. *See* Nuffield, Lord
"Most-favoured-nation" clause, 62, 127
Mussolini, 167–8, 190, 191, 197

"National" or all-party government: experiment of, 9, 13, 15; formation of first, 25, 26, 27 *et seq.*, 41, 48–9; the second, 50 *et seq.*
National Debt, 35, 74, 76, 77
National finance, 73 *et seq.*
National Labour candidates, 46, 49, 54
Naval Conference, 178, 185
Nazis, 66, 167, 183, 184
New York Stock Exchange crash (1929), 13, 21, 22
Nuffield, Lord (Sir W. Morris), 123

Ottawa Agreements, 53–4, 56, 70, 126, 134, 143–60, 190
Ouchy Convention, 62, 63

Paper money, 11
Peace Ballot, 188, 191
Potato Marketing Board, 139
Prices, rise of, 11
Protection, 118 *et seq.*
Protection and Unemployment, 110–24
Protectionist policy, 98 *et seq.*, 117
Public Assistance, 89, 111

"Quotas," 61, 63, 64, 127, 137

Rates and rating, 18, 19, 20
Road Fund, 20, 75
Roosevelt, President, 180, 184
Runciman, W., 42; Runciman Agreements, 152

Samuel, Sir H., 25, 29, 30, 47
Scandinavian countries, 62
Silk Industry, 120
Simon, Sir J., 37, 46, 47, 154, 175, 177, 178, 184, 185, 188
Simonites, 46, 47, 49, 51, 54, 146
Smith, Adam, 37
Snowden, Lord, 21, 42, 44, 48, 53, 54
South Africa. *See* Africa
Stewart, Mr. Malcolm, 96
Sugar Beet subsidy, 20, 134, 135

Tariff Commission, 122, 123
Tariffs, 10, 13, 36, 44, 45, 51, 52, 53, 56, 58, 61, 62, 63, 78, 79, 98, 119, 124
Taxation, 66, 80
Thomas, Mr. J. H., 69
Trade Union leaders, 25

Unemployment, 17, 18, 19, 20, 21, 23, 24, 25, 30, 31, 34, 35, 36, 55, 56, 82, 83, 110–24
Unemployment Assistance Board, 90, 91, 92
Unemployment Insurance Scheme, 17, 30, 35, 51, 64, 65, 87, 88
Unemployment policy, 86 *et seq.*

United States, 9, 11, 12, 13, 14, 22, 61, 74, 75, 76

War Loan, 35, 43, 44, 51, 52, 73, 74, 76, 83
"Wheat quota," 52
Wheat subsidy, 135–6
Workmen's Compensation, 90

Young scheme, the, 166